"Life is fragile! And when tragedy strikes, coping with the realities can be a devastating process. When we are called to navigate the brokenness of life, we need partners who will help us on the journey, and there's no better partner than someone who has walked the journey before us. Thanks to Debbie Mayer for her honest and insightful reflections on her personal experience."

DR. JOSEPH M. STOWELL
President, Cornerstone University, Grand Rapids, Michigan

"Debbie Mayer has not only lived through an unfathomable tragedy, she has emerged out of the ashes with an even deeper faith and a more intimate walk with God. This dear woman of God has a story to tell. I already knew Debbie's story before I picked up her book. But she writes with such intensity and attention to detail, I could not put it down. If you are walking through a valley of your own and if it feels like God has lost your address, read through the pages of this book. God loves you, He's with you, and one day, He'll turn your sorrow into joy."

SUSIE LARSON
Talk Radio Host, National Speaker, Author, *Your Powerful Prayers*

"*After the Crash* is Debbie Mayer's compelling account of God's amazing power to faithfully keep and sustain his children in the midst of immense loss, grief, sorrow, pain, and disappointment. A road no one would choose, but a road some of God's dearly loved ones are entrusted to walk. Debbie's story shows us that even in the midst of suffering, there is still a gracious, good, and loving God who comforts the brokenhearted and promises to never leave us nor forsake us. Walk through the fire with Debbie as she openly shares her struggles of loss and grief, leaning on the strong arms of Jesus, the One who suffered and died for her and promises one day to wipe away all tears. When I think of God's power to sustain in the midst of suffering, I think of my dear friends Joe and Deb Mayer."

STEW LINDBERG
Senior Pastor of Vine Church, Minneapolis, Minnesota

A TRUE STORY

AFTER THE
CRASH

Grieving With Hope in
Light of Eternity

Debbie L Mayer

AFTER THE CRASH: Grieving with Hope in Light of Eternity

Copyright © 2017 Debbie L. Mayer

ISBN 978-0-9982400-1-5

Edited by Peter Lundell (www.peterlundell.com)

Additional edits by Margaret Montreuil (www.margaretmontreuil.com)

Proofread by Christy Distler (www.aspireeditingservices.com)

Cover design by Joey Mayer

Interior Design by Katherine Lloyd (www.thedeskonline.com)

Author Photo by Megan Murray

DLM logo by David Byrd (davidbyrd.com)

Printed in the United States of America

Smith Printing

17343 Wolverine Street NW, Ramsey, MN 55303

1-800-416-9099 • www.SmithPrinting.net

17 18 19 20 21 5 4 3 2 1

In loving memory of
Krista Joy, Nikki Ann, and Jessica Lynn Mayer
Your lives spoke and continue to speak
to all you touched with each unique expression
of God's love that He placed in you.
I love and miss you so much!
"Love never fails."
–1 Corinthians 13:8

Dedicated to
Joey, Bree, and Vivien
Watching you embrace God and His goodness
has brought me more joy than you know.
May the dreams God has placed in your hearts come true.
I love you!

Joe
My husband, best friend, confidant, and counselor
who always calls me back to life and love.
I cannot fathom life without you.
I love you!

Acknowledgments

Thank you to my friends and family who have walked by my side on this grief journey, and who have encouraged and cheered me on to obey the voice of God in the writing of this book. Thank you, brother David, for getting me going with your questions, feedback, and ideas that helped me think about what I was writing. Thank you to Ken & Patty Freeman and Char Montag for reading and re-reading, and for your never-ending positive feedback, love, and prayer.

Thank you to all who financially gave to make this book possible, and to all who supported me with prayer. There are really too many people in these lists to mention all of you, but please know that I'm eternally grateful for your gifts of love, support, and finances. I could not have done this without all of you.

Thank you to all the new friends I have met along the way who have so graciously and generously offered your time, expertise and help.

Thank you, Peter, for your intense honesty, objectivity, ideas, and skill. Thank you, Margaret, for both your sacrifice and generosity of time. Thank you to Anne Shannon, my good neighbor, for contributing your time, support, and skill in the layout of the photographs.

David Sluka, thank you for going the extra mile in extending your kindness, time, and advice.

Thank you, Katherine and Christy for being so patient, helpful, and understanding.

Most of all, I want to thank the Lord for the direction, help, healing, and provision He has abundantly poured out on me and my sincere gratitude for His unfailing truth and never ending love.

Contents

Foreword xi

Part One: GONE

1. All Three? 3

Part Two: BUILT ON THE ROCK

2. Enduring Foundation 11
3. The House That God Built 15

Part Three: THE STORM

4. Have Yourself a Merry Little Christmas 33
5. What Am I Going to Do? 42
6. Tokens From Heaven 49
7. Beautiful Departure 56
8. Carried 63
9. Through Heaven's Eyes 69
10. Almost There 77
11. Three Brides In Heaven 82
12. It Takes a Body 92

Part Four: NAVIGATING THE WAVE

13. Eye of the Storm 103
14. In the Aftermath 112

15. One Step at a Time 122
16. Snapshots, Videos, Cassette Tapes, and Memories 130
17. Memorials to God's Power and Presence 137
18. Strength In Weakness. 144
19. Green Pastures and Still Waters 151
20. Walking Through the Shadowlands 158

Part Five: DARKNESS BEFORE DAWN

21. Veiled Perspective. 167
22. Darkness. 173
23. Remembering the Signs 181
24. Signs of Hope. 189
25. Will the Real Debbie Please Stand Up? 197

Part Six: PRESSING ON

26. Embracing Life 207
27. I Bow Down 211
28. My House Still Stands 216
29. The Bride of Christ. 221
30. Still Being Written 228

Notes 239

Foreword

I clearly remember the moment we received the phone call. It was unbelievably hard to grasp. Three beautiful young lives tragically ended. In an instant, Sandi and I cried out to God in our own anguish. Quickly we regrouped and jumped into the car to go to Joe and Debbie. How would we respond to the deep pain we would meet when their door opened? Quite honestly, all we could do is to continue to cry and pray.

To our wonder, when the door opened, we came face to face with two people ... our brother and sister in Christ, who really were *in Christ* in the deepest way we had ever seen. Eternity became so real ... so tangible ... so immediate!

Yes, they were in deep grief, but the presence of God supernaturally manifested in the room. It seemed like you could reach out and physically touch Him. Every breath seemed to inhale the Holy Spirit and exhale the hope of heaven. They (and we) knew the embrace of the Father's grace and His healing love that changes everything.

To the natural mind, this would have seemed like it was the end. How could life go on for anyone after such apparent and tragic loss? Billy Graham once said, "When we come to the end of ourselves, that is the beginning of God." For Joe and Debbie, that is a day by day reality.

After the crash, something happened. Let me rephrase that. They *allowed* something to happen. They allowed the Shepherd to lead them through this valley of death into the tangible fullness of knowing firsthand the experience of eternal life. This began a process. A process for both Debbie and Joe. Yes, this wasn't the end but the beginning. The beginning of a painful but life-giving process of allowing the Father to reveal to them the certainty that their daughters were in His arms in heaven, and that they, Joe and Debbie, were in His arms on earth. As Joe said, "How could I be angry at God when my daughters were experiencing the fulness of the Father's love?"

Jesus said, "Anyone who listens to my teaching and follows it is wise, like a person who builds a house on solid rock. Though the rain comes in torrents and the floodwaters rise and the winds beat against that house, it won't collapse because it is built on bedrock" (Matthew 7:24–25 NLT). And in Isaiah we read, "But LORD, be merciful to us, for we have waited for you. Be our strong arm each day and our salvation in times of trouble. ... In that day he will be your sure foundation, providing a rich store of salvation, wisdom, and knowledge. The fear of the LORD will be your treasure" (Isaiah 33:2, 6 NLT).

The truth is that sometimes we don't realize how deep our foundation in Christ is, until the storm comes. And we all go through storms. When things have collapsed, at least in our natural perception, the treasure of knowing that God truly heals the broken-hearted can begin to be grasped. Trusting in God at those times is what makes us realize that He is our treasure. As we treasure God in those times, we learn to trust Him with everything ... and in everything.

I am convinced this book is for everyone who's going through the heartache of mourning. Oh, I know that you and I probably cannot begin to know the depth of grief that the Mayers have experienced. But in some sense, most of us have experienced some kind of "crash." The crash of a failed relationship, divorce, broken dream, sickness, financial loss, and even the aftermath of darkness of the soul that comes from a loss of fulfillment.

This is more than just one family's story, and it clearly articulates the moment-by-moment, day-by-day pain and struggle that comes into the heart of anyone who goes through tragedy and loss. In this book, Debbie takes us on her intensely personal journey through extreme grief into the embrace of God's grace. I recommend that you read it almost like a daily devotional. Take your time with the emotions and the moments. Let the healing balm of God's love rest in your heart as it did in Joe's and Debbie's. The thoughts that are written, and the journey that is recorded, will resonate within your heart and guide you through your own journey into healing and wholeness.

Pastor Mike Smith
Redeeming Love Church
Maplewood, Minnesota
Minnesota Senate Chaplain

Part One

GONE

Chapter 1

All Three?

You are a story.
You are not merely the possessor and teller of a number of stories;
You are a well-written and intentional story that is authored by
the Greatest Writer of all time, and before time and after time.
—To Be Told by Dan Allender

One day left.

The new year had come, January 1, 2004. Waking up New Year's morning, I felt an extra tug for God's presence, anticipating my son's wedding in just a couple of days. It had been a busy Christmas and I longed for a bit of quiet. After spending some time reading my Bible, I asked my husband, Joe, if we could pray together. We had been hosting out-of-town family for the Christmas holidays and the upcoming wedding. As we held hands, we asked God to glorify Himself no matter what, through laughter or tears. That seemed like a strange way to pray for a wedding, yet those were my exact words.

Through laughter or tears.

I prepared a brunch for those staying with us and in nearby hotels. After eating, we played a board game and continued visiting. Jessica, my youngest daughter, eager to entertain, told a joke she'd learned from Joe. No matter how often she told it, she could never tell it without laughing before the punch line. I think we laughed more at her uncontrolled laughter than the joke itself.

Seven hours left.

All three girls were to be bridesmaids in their big brother's wedding. What an exciting way to bring in the new year. They would soon make the two-hour drive to Willmar, Minnesota, where the wedding would be held. The plan was to meet up with Bree, their future sister-in-law, and the other bridesmaids at the Green Mill for dinner and a night of girl fun.

Krista, my oldest daughter, left for her apartment to get ready and gather the goodies she and I had made for the hospitality baskets to set in our guests' hotel rooms. "I'll be back in a little bit. Peace out, Mama!" she said as she pranced out the door.

Nikki, my middle daughter, took a shower and came out wearing one of her new pink sweaters, curiously posing. "So how do I look, Mom?"

"Oh, you look pretty in pink, Nik."

Four hours left.

The process of letting Joey go had been challenging for me. My first child to get married meant the beginning of a new season of life, not only for him but for me as well. He wasn't just my only son; he was my oldest child, and we had a special bond. In a way, I grew up alongside him as I practiced my newfound skills of parenting.

Over the years, I had learned to process my feelings through songwriting, so I applied that practice to this season as well, jotting down memories of younger years with Joey. My girls heard endless laments of how hard the process was for me, and even helped with some of the lyrics as they reminisced about growing up. It seemed like only yesterday when I sent him off to kindergarten, and then to Teens Missions for an entire month the summer he was eleven. Now his wedding day was approaching all too fast for this emotional mama!

Krista, trying to encourage me, often reminded me that I wasn't losing a son but gaining a daughter, just as she was gaining a sister.

So my self-therapy had begun as I wrote my letting-go song. I titled it "Seems Like Only Yesterday."

With each memory, happy and sad tears dropped to the pages. Halfway into my writing, I decided I wanted to sing it for Joey on his wedding day, but I needed to know if he'd like me to. After I asked him, he smiled and said, "Sure, Mom. Why don't you sing it at the reception?"

After that, the two of us prayed, asking God to glorify Himself through the events of the next few days. Exciting time as it was, I would have to let go of our relationship as I knew it.

Let go.

When we finished praying, Joey handed me a painting that Bree had received while touring that summer with One Accord, the worship band that represented North Central Bible College, where they attended. It was a picture of a bride and groom representing Jesus and His bride, the church.

Something inside me jumped when I saw it. "Thank you," I said and set it aside, unaware of the significant theme and impact it would soon have on my life.

By this time, Krista had returned and Nikki had gassed up the car. Nikki was the first one out the door after giving me a hug. "Bye, Mom! See you tomorrow!"

Jess was right behind her, excited to go. Just two days earlier, my mom and I had taken Jess to get her hair and nails done—her first time to experience that kind of pampering. Soon she would be wearing the bridesmaid dress she had modeled for her best friend two days earlier, complemented by her fancy nails and hair. Such excitement for a twelve-year-old girl. As she walked out the door, her one hand embraced her *The Lord of the Rings* book received for Christmas and her other clung to her trusty childhood blanket.

"Bye, Mom!" We hugged and she walked out the door.

As Krista left, she asked me to dry the few pieces of laundry she had thrown in the washing machine and bring them with me the next day, along with their bridesmaid dresses. While stepping out the door, she sheepishly added, "Oh, and Mom, could you iron the dresses too?"

I paused, rolled my eyes, and laughed. "Sure." *As if I didn't have enough to do.*

Joe followed them outside, gave each one a hug, and said goodbye. Goodbye.

Two hours left.

Joey left soon after the girls to pick up Jordan, his best man, at the Minneapolis airport. Before heading to Willmar, they stopped by our house so Jordan could say a quick hello. They had been friends since kindergarten, so Jordan knew us quite well. Before they left for Joey's apartment to gather his stuff, Joey said with his voice full of anticipation, "See you tomorrow night at the rehearsal dinner."

"Yeah, see you tomorrow night, Mr. and Mrs. Mayer," echoed Jordan.

My younger brother David and his family, who were staying with us, also left for the evening to take in dinner and a movie in order to give Joe and me a much-needed break. Finally—the house was quiet and we had some time alone.

Thirty minutes left.

I started ironing the dresses but felt so tired and, although it was only 6:30 p.m., I put on my pajamas. I felt strange. Even a little depressed. I figured I was just exhausted from the holidays and all the company. Despite feeling drained, I began packing things to bring to Willmar the next day.

With a weird sense of apprehension, I said to Joe, "Something is not right here."

We said a prayer, committing everything to God once again. I called my sister Patty, who was then staying with other family members, to make sure they all knew the directions to the church. And I asked for prayer.

No time left.

As I packed, Bree called, asking if we had heard from the girls. She told us they'd called her around 6:00 p.m., saying they would be there in a half an hour. It was now 8:00 p.m. and they still weren't there. I wasn't sure if I should be upset with the girls or worried. I figured—and secretly hoped—they had just stopped for coffee and lost track of time. That wouldn't be unusual for them. Bree had called their cell phones with no response. Now, in hopes they had just missed her call, we also called. No one answered.

By this time, my heart pounded so hard I could not ignore my anxious thoughts, but I tried not to think the worst. Feeling alarmed, I called Patty back and asked her to pray again. I emphatically told her that I was *not* going to give in to fear. Everything would be all right.

After she prayed with me, I went to the basement and began to nervously fold Krista's dried clothes. I collapsed onto the cold basement floor and cried out to God, "I can't do this!"

I didn't even know what I was saying I couldn't do. I felt just sick with fear. Whatever was happening, I was fully aware I could not handle it myself. Then I told God I was sorry. "Not my will, but let Your will be done." In spite of my intense uneasiness, I knew God was with me.

Bree called back to say she had been informed that there had been an accident involving three girls who had been admitted to the hospital, and that a state trooper was being sent to talk with her.

I felt paralyzed.

Joe called the state patrol and got no information. After receiving another call from Bree, he decided to call Rice Memorial Hospital in Willmar. He was on the phone while sitting at our kitchen table when I came up from the basement. Standing about fifteen feet from him, I heard the voice from the other end of the receiver say the words *medical examiner.*

I screamed.

Joe slowly asked, "All three?"

Part Two

BUILT ON THE ROCK

~~ Chapter 2 ~~

Enduring Foundation

Let me hear Thee speaking in my heart.
Let me get used to the sound of Thy voice, that its tones
may be familiar when the sounds of earth die away and
the only sound will be the music of Thy speaking voice. Amen.
—*THE PURSUIT OF GOD* BY A. W. TOZER

Every relationship has a series of past encounters and events that make the relationship what it is today. Our history with God is the most important in any of our relationships.

No one is immune to the horrors and tribulations that can come upon us due to the condition of our fallen world and the enemy of God. Jesus lovingly warned us that storms would come, but He promised in His Word that we would find comfort in Him. "I have told you these things, so that in me you may have peace. In this world you will have trouble. But take heart! I have overcome the world" (John 16:33). Because of God's grace and my foundation in Him, I would miraculously survive the violent storm that would hit my life.

Understanding each other is foundational in any close relationship. From the beginning, God revealed His heart to me in ways I could understand because He speaks my language. It didn't prevent the storm from coming, but it made the difference between surviving or being totally wiped out.

I grew up knowing about Jesus because my family attended and was involved at church. He was, when I was very young, the One I sang about: "What a Friend we have in Jesus, all our sins and grief to bear. What a privilege to carry everything to God in prayer." My very best friend. I had a sense in my young heart and mind that Jesus loved being with me.

By the time I was a teenager though, church no longer interested me. During elementary and junior high school, I had experienced rejection to the point that I felt like a loser much of the time. My heart and self-worth were further damaged when my boyfriend, who was a little older than me, broke up with me in my junior year of high school and soon after married an acquaintance of mine. Again, the "loser" in me questioned if I was too ugly, too fat, or just not enjoyable to be around.

God was no longer a major part of my life by the time I attended the University of Minnesota and worked as a waitress at a restaurant near the campus. By then I had a hefty smoking habit, drank every weekend, and experimented with several drugs.

Often, when I waited for a city bus, I watched a girl who stood on the corner, passing out gospel tracts. Each time I glanced at her, she would smile and say, "God is Love!" and offer me a message of God's salvation. I pegged her as a religious fanatic, but at the same time, her eyes seemed to pour out love as she spoke. I found myself disappointed if I didn't see her.

The girl was kind enough to smile at me and tell me God loved me, caring about me regardless of how I negatively responded to her. More than once after I had seen her, I took a seat on the bus and the graffiti-covered back of the seat in front of me stared back with the words *God loves you!* Also, in a restroom at the university, the words *God is Love* sprawled across the wall in big red letters. I saw the same words painted on the sides of buildings, on park benches, on bridges, and again on the back of a seat on a bus. Talk about the "writing on the wall." God pursued me, making sure I'd get His message everywhere I turned. He wants all of us to get it. It's not meant to be a mystery.

I'd often smoke my last cigarette of the day, climb into bed, and think of heaven and hell. I carried guilt and shame as heavy weights. When all was quiet and I was alone, I couldn't ignore the nagging questions. *When will I die? Where will I go? Will I ever change? Will I ever find true love?* I had done so many wrong things—things I told myself I would never do. I knew in my head God loved me, but the truth hadn't made it into my heart. In fact, the loudest voice in my head called me a *big loser.*

The enemy of my soul attacked my emotional weakness, intending to brand me with the lie that I was not lovable. He attempted to keep me from knowing and experiencing God's love. The Bible speaks of the devil as the accuser of the brethren, a liar and a thief who comes to steal, kill, and destroy (John 10:10). He attempted to stifle my discovery of the only truth that could set me free. That's his goal with anyone.

On a Sunday night in October 1977, my sister Patty invited me to a place called Jesus People Church. I had visited there before, but that night changed my life. All day I had anticipated that something good might happen. When I was there, the people around me sang love songs to God with passion and joy. I longed for what they had. Then the pastor invited anyone who wanted to know God's love to come forward and pray.

I stood in place, struggling with myself. *Boy, I would love to have what these people have, but I smoke and I can't quit. I don't think I'd make a very good Christian. I'd better wait till I quit.*

The music kept playing and the invitation continued. Then another thought came into my head: *I will lose all my friends.* Having friends was a huge measurement of how lovable I was, a carryover from my childhood rejection and insecurity.

As I dwelled on these thoughts, the pastor lifted his voice and said, "There's someone out there who is thinking you will never be able to quit that habit and that you will lose all your friends."

My heart pounded. *He's talking about me!*

He added, "God loves you just where you're at and takes you just as you are. If you lose friends because you choose what's right, they're not the kind of friends you want anyway. Besides, Jesus is the best friend you could ever have." The pastor went on to explain that there was nothing I could do to earn my salvation and that Jesus did it all on the cross; I just had to receive it as a free gift.

I found myself stepping into the aisle with tears streaming down my face. I felt light and loved. I knew everything dark that I had done—and was so ashamed of—was forgiven. My guilt washed away. I knew the God of the universe loved me enough to send His Son to die for me. I stood straighter than before. I cried cleansing tears for quite a while. I felt clean. And new.

That was the beginning of my extraordinary love journey—my relationship with God.

The Old Testament describes friends of God as those who "walked with God." I became one of them. Everything changed in me. And, believe it or not, God delivered me from smoking cigarettes that night. I lost desire for a lot of the things of my old lifestyle. I had a new heart; and now, after my unsuccessful pursuit of love in all the wrong places, at age twenty-one, I became a new creation. "Therefore, if anyone is in Christ, the new creation has come: The old has gone, the new is here!" (2 Corinthians 5:17).

I wanted to please Jesus. This felt natural because my inner being had changed, including what I wanted to do. I experienced freedom, purpose, and joy like never before. I wanted to follow the promptings I felt were from the Holy Spirit, because now I was in Christ with new goals in life.

I started regularly attending Jesus People Church in downtown Minneapolis. The insecure, stifled, and cynical Debbie began a new chapter in her history with God.

Chapter 3

The House That God Built

A family is where life begins and love never ends.
—AUTHOR UNKNOWN

What an exciting time of life it was. Each day I learned new things about this God who loved me even before I loved Him. I began to realize more and more that what matters is what Christ did for me, not what I could do for Him. Being His had nothing to do with my performance.

I visited a place called Park House—a discipleship home for young people who could live, learn, and practice the disciplines of Christian living while in community together. I started attending their weekly Bible study, met the people who lived there, and decided this was where I wanted to be—at least for a while. Park House consisted of two homes: one for girls and one for guys, located a block apart.

The day I moved in, I met Joe. I was immediately drawn to his quiet, gentle way, and quickly discovered he was one of the kindest and wisest people I would ever know. We worked at Jesus People Church and drove to work together, saw each other throughout the day, and ate dinner together with other members of Park House. He worked as a janitor for the church campus, and I became the errand-runner. At the end of my hectic run of errands, he would often end up praying for me. I began to apply Scripture to my everyday life, gaining the wisdom I needed to begin responding to my circumstances and relationships in a healthy way. I discovered what, and how much, God thought of me.

At age thirteen, I had received my first guitar and began to process my feelings through songwriting, but music became even more precious to me at this time in my life. The first song I wrote as a new believer was "Jesus, Sweet Jesus," also the first song I ever sang at church.

> Jesus, sweet Jesus. Jesus, sweet Jesus.
> You've got that loving power!
> I was waiting for someone to come into my life to love.
> I was searching high and low; but little did I know
> That You've been loving me before I even knew,
> You had your hand on my life
> But I was too busy living for myself that
> I passed Your sweet love by.

I soon discovered that fearing God meant more than simply respecting Him and that our relationship with Him involves being aware of His constant presence: "The Lord confides in those who fear him; he makes his covenant known to them" (Psalm 25:14). I began to experience what it meant to practically "walk with God"—including what it's like to converse with this Friend. Like in any relationship, conversations with someone often make a lasting impression on you, and in this case that Someone was God.

When we're aware of God's presence, we will hear His faintest whispers. If we seek His wisdom in the Bible, the Holy Spirit will share God's secrets with us. God revealed Himself and His heart to me, and it amazed me that He confided in me. Just ordinary me. I wasn't anybody special, but He is no respecter of persons and, to Him, I am special.

I eagerly listened.

Through biblical knowledge, experiences, and conversations with God, six core truths became the foundation stones on which I built my faith and relationship with God. The first truth was about God's heart—He *wants* a relationship with me.

Number one core foundation stone: God wants to share His secrets with me—He is my Best Friend.

While I lived at Park House, a group of friends did a Bible study on the bride of Christ. Until then, I had never heard the phrase. Astonished, I learned about the intimate relationship God designed and wants us to have with Him. This divine romance theme captured my heart and came to identify me as His bride for all eternity. I learned that He rejoices over me: "As a bridegroom rejoices over his bride, so will your God rejoice over you" (Isaiah 62:5b). Other Scriptures taught me how much God delights in me and that He even sings over me. Although I could hardly comprehend this in reality, I loved it. This was an important truth God gave me early on in our relationship.

Number two core foundation stone: I am the bride of Christ— He's my Bridegroom.

While still at Park House, I read about enduring trials, and still more about God's love popped out at me: "Blessed is the man who remains steadfast under trial, for when he has stood the test he will receive the crown of life, which God has promised to those who love Him" (James 1:12). A margin note in my Bible referred to this crown of life as the "lover's crown." That popped off the page at me. My strength to endure to the end would come by the love of God. Without it, trials could cause me to become bitter and critical, losing not my salvation but this lover's crown. Only those believers who love God more than life itself will receive the lover's crown. God gave me another key truth that would carry me often the rest of my life.

Number three core foundation stone: As I endure trials, I will receive the lover's crown—for God is my eternal reward.

These themes of intimacy and relationship transformed how I understood, not only Christianity but also who I am. I was created for an intimate love relationship with God.

After some time, I was quite sure Joe was the man I would marry. But after dating for nearly six months, he drove me home from church one night and was extra quiet. After coming to a stop in front of my apartment, he told me he really cared about me, but . . .

But. He hardly had to say more. Out of courtesy for him, I quietly waited for him finish.

"But . . . at this point I'm not ready to commit to anything long-term."

I blinked back tears. I didn't want to hear these words and yet, somehow, I knew in my spirit, he had to say them. The human side of me felt as if my heart had been ripped out. My feelings said, *I remember this pain.* But my spirit had a faint assurance that God was working in this.

The following week I wrote in my journal, "I feel if I stop crying, I will die." I felt so rejected. Again. It went deep. My past hurts rose to the surface.

Even so, I knew something had to happen. The way things were going, we needed to move ahead or stop seeing each other. We had broken up, and I desperately needed to know how to deal with my feelings.

I asked God to give me hope—to speak to me. I read, "Whom have I in heaven but you? And earth has nothing I desire besides you. My flesh and my heart may fail, but God is the strength of my heart and my portion forever" (Psalm 73:25–26).

God showed me that night that I had been looking to Joe to give me what only God could give. He wanted me to know that my foundation must be solely on the Rock, Jesus Christ, and not on any human being. Not even Joe. I told God I was sorry for putting Joe first. I sensed God saying that human beings will fail me, even the best of them. But He will never fail me. I soon realized my first love and desire truly was Jesus, and He alone was more than enough for me. This settled my heart; I needed nothing more.

I knew God was with me and that He alone could satisfy my soul. I had my next core truth to base my life on.

Number four core foundation stone: God wants to be number one in my heart—He is my portion forever.

Because of Joe's own life struggles at that time, he needed to know if he really loved me and not just the fact that someone loved him. After a lot of soul searching, he concluded that I was too precious to lose because of his fear.

Just one week after our breakup, he so sweetly recited to me the gentle, positive phrase he had heard in his mind throughout the week: *Jesus, Joe, and Debbie.* After hearing that phrase, he said it all made sense to him. It sounded right to me too!

Before either of us could arrive at that conclusion though, we each needed to go through our own struggle to discover the proper hierarchy of relationship in our hearts: Jesus first, then each other, then ourselves.

Six months later we were married. God's truth was the foundation of our lives and love. The theme for our wedding was "His truth has set us free to love," based on John 8:32: "Then you will know the truth, and the truth will set you free." I wrote and recorded a song for our wedding, "I Love You!" which we played before we said our vows.

> I love you because God gave you to me.
> I love you with a love so pure and free.
> These are the things God said are love …
>
> Love is gentle, Love is kind,
> Love is patient; Love is yours and mine.
> Love is tender, Love is not blind,
> the Love Jesus gives is not the hurting kind.
>
> You know Jesus gave His Love to you and me,
> so we could lift up His name for all eternity
> And now the union of our spirits here might help others to see
> that love's not just a feeling;
> but the Person who lives in you and me.
> His name is Jesus. His name is Jesus. His name is Jesus!

Joe and Debbie, dating – 1979

Joe and Debbie, engaged – 1979

Joe and Debbie's wedding day –
June 14th, 1980

It's a boy!

In September 1981, our first child, Joseph Martin Mayer, was born. We named him Joseph after the Joes before him—his dad, grandpa, and great-grandpa. His middle name, Martin, came from my maternal grandpa. Joseph means "God will increase." I had wanted a little boy and loved him so much.

Time and time again I'd look at Joey in wonder that he came from Joe and me. From the moment we brought him home from the hospital, he was all boy and full of energy. The first night home, I held him in my arms while pacing around our apartment into the wee hours of the night, trying to get him to fall asleep. He propped his head on my shoulder, alert and eager to check out his new home, not wanting to miss a thing. He studied his new surroundings with the same tenacity, curiosity, and sense of adventure he still has today.

As a toddler, he was especially playful, learning with each new experience, eager to show off every newfound skill. He was a little person always on the go, passionately discovering the world around him. Not only was he on the go, but he was also very sensitive to the things of God. He loved to pray and ask God to move in people's lives.

It's a girl!

Two and half years later, in April 1984, more joy came when Krista Joy arrived. Krista means "follower of Christ." Her middle name is Joy because my pregnancy with her was just that, full of joy.

Even when I went into labor with her, we laughed the entire way to the hospital. Unlike my first labor, during which I never noticed my water breaking, with Krista my water broke at home, requiring me to change my clothes twice, only to discover I was still drenched in the car. We could not stop laughing! Perhaps that is one reason she was so lighthearted growing up. She always found crazy ways to make us laugh.

I loved having a little girl. Her easygoing and complacent personality balanced her big brother's tenacity and energy.

Krista contentedly played with her dolls and other toys and was affectionate and relational. Because of her loving, gentle nature, she became everybody's sweetheart, winning the heart of whomever she was around. Something about Krista made a person want to be near her, even when she became a teenager and young adult.

Another girl!

Two years later, in March 1986, came Nikki Ann. Nikki was induced and born in a quick forty-five minutes. But we couldn't bring her home right away. She spent the first ten days of her new life in the hospital because of transient tachypnea, a condition in which fluid remains in the baby's lungs. It was difficult for Nikki to inhale oxygen properly, so she had to breathe faster and harder to get enough air into her lungs. She needed to be monitored and take antibiotics, but she came home a healthy baby, full of determination.

She definitely knew what she did and did not like. We didn't name her for two days, until Joe came up with Nikki, which appropriately means "victorious heart." Ann is my mother's middle name.

Nikki arrived home to a wall of artwork that Joey and Krista had enthusiastically colored and taped above her bassinet to inform her how much she was loved. She always loved the attention of her older siblings, especially her big brother. Whenever Joey came near her, she grinned from ear to ear. He had a way of calming her down whenever she cried.

Nikki was our quiet, reflective, more serious child. Even as a toddler she had a sharp mind and sensitive spirit. Before she could read, she was often content to look at books, making up an entire story while looking at the pictures.

Joey and Krista enjoyed playing with her, dressing her up, and treating her like a doll. They'd feed her and then laugh because she made a mess while making funny faces.

Still another girl!

Five years after Nikki, in February 1991, we were pleasantly surprised by Jessica Lynn. Joe came up with her name too. It means "God's gift" or "wealth," appropriate because she was an unexpected gift. Lynn is my middle name.

Jessica began entertaining us at two weeks of age, which continued to unfold as part of her personality. She had no problem being in the spotlight as she discovered how we all loved her performances. As a toddler, she memorized songs from the Barney and Psalty videos she watched daily. Excitedly, she'd sit us all down to watch her perform. She performed the well-rehearsed choreography for each song she sang, and eagerly obliged as we captured her on film.

Joey, Krista, and Nikki fought over who would get to hold her. They adored her. She was lovable with a contagious little giggle that made us smile and want to squeeze her. She quickly acquired the nickname of "tippy-toe girl" because she walked on her tiptoes.

I absolutely loved being a mother and caring for my family. Joe was a kind and patient husband and father. We experienced our ups and downs, laughter and tears, but the foundation God laid for our lives could not be shaken. We knew nothing of the storm that would one day sweep over our lives, ultimately demonstrating the powerful reality of the truth of God's love.

A house might be big or small, new or old, but what lies underneath any house, largely out of sight, is the most important part—the foundation on which the house rests. The same is true with a family.

Matthew 7:24 speaks of building one's spiritual house on a rock, which is itself the strongest of foundations. In building our family, we used rock-solid footings that became our foundation in faith:

1. A living relationship with the Lord Jesus Christ and one another
2. The Word of God

Joseph Martin – 1981

Joey, nine years old

Krista Joy – 1984

Krista, eight years old

Nikki Ann – 1986

Nikki, ten years old

Jessica Lynn – 1991

Jessica, nine years old

3. Prayer
4. Church family (community)

God's supernatural love, which is the "perfect bond of unity" (Colossians 3:14) is the concrete that held, and still holds, our family together.

We read and endeavored to memorize Scripture with our children. We prayed together and were committed and involved at our church, dedicated to growing in God's love. Valuing the relationships and input of our family and friends, we were thankful to each of them for speaking into our lives. The African proverb "It takes a village to raise a child" is so true. We were not meant to go this journey of raising a family alone. We were created for community.

Throughout life, it's important to keep doing what you know is right for your journey, trusting the map even if it doesn't look familiar. Our map was the Bible, and we did our best to obey its teachings even when the way was unfamiliar. Sometimes there would have been easier routes to take, at least in the short term, but it costs something to obey God's Word. At times it created friction between Joe and me or between us and the kids. Sometimes even family or friends didn't understand our choices.

Who doesn't love the times on a road trip when the scenery is breathtaking and everyone is happy? Unfortunately, that's not always the case, and neither is our life journey. Sometimes the scenery is boring or even ugly. We can become so focused on following routes that we forget to gas up or change the oil. But a car can't run on fumes, and neither can a family.

As we attempted to follow Jesus Christ and serve Him as a family, we struggled along the way just like any other family. Those became times for maintenance and repair.

I faced some inner struggles during a two-year period of homeschooling the kids, which brought up old insecurity issues in me. Along with some situations with family and friends, this made me feel like a failure. The deeper reality was that God allowed these feelings to surface so I could face and overcome some lifelong insecurities—learning to find my worth not in what I do, but in who I am and what

God says about me. He wanted to drive that into my soul, to establish deeper and stronger footings to my foundation, so I could extend that to my children as well.

During this time of family and personal reconditioning, we also renovated our bathroom. We lived in an old house that had layer upon layer of old wallpaper and paint. The first task was to strip all of it off, which took long-term commitment. After I had stripped most of it, a friend of Krista's was over and said, "Eesh! I liked it better before!"

I laughed because I felt the same way about our life circumstances. I am so thankful I didn't believe that lie and end up settling for just looking okay on the outside. I'm glad God strips us of our old ways, layer by layer, to get to the natural beauty He's created in us, which usually takes a lifetime.

A few days after Krista's friend's remark, Joey was helping me strip the rest of the woodwork. "Mom, this is really messy."

"It sure is. But it's going to look great when we're done."

"But it's taking such a long time."

I laughed and thought, *Isn't that the truth!*

The project seemed like it would never end. But I knew what I wanted it to look like, and that it would be beautiful when completed. I wanted people to see it in its messy condition so they could see the transformation when the bathroom was finished.

Then a light bulb went on for me. I thought about our circumstances and life in general. We really shouldn't be embarrassed about what we go through and what God is doing in us. He sees us not as we are, but as we will be. He's the Master Craftsman. Change seems to take forever, but He knows exactly what He's doing and will finish little by little and in His time. I am confident and know that He who began a good work in me will carry it on to completion until the day of Christ Jesus.

Our bathroom took more than a year to finish, but finish it I did—and I loved it. So did Krista's friend. And as for our family, God continued doing maintenance, repairs, and upgrades. We were messy at times, and the changes seemed to take forever. But He was building on the firm foundation that had already been laid, and I loved every improvement—that is, after the job was completed.

However, while in the process of renovation, this period of turmoil brought more insecurities to a head, and I felt panicky and alone, as if I were drowning. It was like a time I body-surfed in the ocean. I had been caught in a wave and struggled to come up from under water. Just like I felt then, I was disoriented and afraid in this time of darkness and trouble. The emotional wave I struggled with was loneliness, fear, and panic from loss of control.

God led me to read Psalm 18:5, 16–19: "In my distress I called to the Lord; I cried to my God for help. From his temple he heard my voice; my cry came before him, into his ears. ... God reached down from on high and took hold of me; he drew me out of deep waters. He rescued me from my powerful enemy, from my foes, who were too strong for me. They confronted me in the day of my disaster, but the Lord was my support. He brought me out into a spacious place; he rescued me because he delighted in me."

I could see God bending down, raising my cries to His ear, and lifting me out of the suffocating waves. And it was all because He delighted in me. I called this my "Surfing Psalm," which brought me to my next core truth.

Number five core foundation stone: God sees, hears, and delights in me—He's the Lover of my soul.

During this same time of feeling overwhelmed, I read the story in 2 Chronicles 20 of King Jehoshaphat and the Israelites, who were facing destruction by armies too big for them: "'For we have no power to face this vast army that is attacking us. We do not know what to do, but our eyes are on you.' ... 'Do not be afraid or discouraged because of this vast army. The battle is not yours, but God's'" (vv. 12, 15). God wanted to set me free from *works* and *striving*. He wrote on my heart that His Word can conquer all opposition in my life. I only need to fix my eyes on Him. Another core truth.

Number six core truth foundation stone: Even when I don't know what to do, God does —He's my Rescuing Savior.

It was then I read Proverbs 24:3–4, "By wisdom a house is built; and through understanding it is established; through knowledge its rooms are filled with rare and beautiful treasures." This verse became my mission statement as a mother and wife.

No two families are alike, so we can't just copy another family that seems to have things together. I wanted my children to be whom God created them to be, not just fit a mold of what I thought they should be. Proverbs 24 promises that the results of this will be a family that offers "rare and beautiful treasures" to the world. But true beauty reflects the character of God and displays His handiwork, not our own goodness. There is no way to fake this. It must be the result of building on the Rock—life's surest foundation. This was something Joe and I regularly sought and prayed for.

Joey, Krista, Nikki, and Jess dressed up
for 1991 World Series

Family photo – 1994

Family photo – 1999

Part Three

THE
STORM

Chapter 4

Have Yourself
a Merry Little Christmas

The best of all gifts around any Christmas tree:
the presence of a happy family all wrapped up in each other.
—Burton Hills

Christmas Eve Day 2003 brought a chilly seventeen degrees according to the outside thermometer. Inside, lively conversations and cheerful singing kept us warm and cozy.

"Through the years we all will be together, if the fates allow ..." sang Krista in her sweet, high voice. Peering through bifocals balanced on the tip of his nose, my dad played the piano and sang along. Mom joined in, "Let your heart be light; from now on our troubles will be out of sight."

I had grown up singing songs around the piano with my family. This was a tradition that made holidays complete for me and a favorite for my kids as well.

Bree gracefully played "Winter Wonderland" as we all joined in and harmonized.

"Good job, Bree!" exclaimed my dad as he admired her skill of sight-reading.

Joey and Bree met a few years earlier at North Central Bible College. Bree's major was Music Performance and Joey's was Pastoral

Studies. People often joke that even if a student doesn't graduate with a degree, they will often walk away with a spouse.

Outside, snow fell, leaving a fresh white blanket on everything. We waited for Joe to come home from work so we could celebrate our first round of Christmas. Every so often Jessica's animated giggles echoed in response to Joey's goofy antics and Krista's comic impersonations.

Jess, age twelve, gradually lost interest in the last few songs. She found more important matters at hand, like investigating which presents were hers. As Joe walked through the door, she exclaimed, "Yeah, Dad's home!" Finally, we could open our gifts and dig into the Christmas cookies.

Jess opened her much-anticipated *The Lord of the Rings* book. She had spent hours getting lost in C. S. Lewis's The Chronicles of Narnia series. Now she was excited to add Tolkien, Lewis's mentor and friend, to her list of read authors. Her next package was a black lacey shirt to match the skirt she'd inherited from Nikki. She modeled the new shirt, and Krista yelled out, "You should wear that to the rehearsal dinner."

"Yeah!" cheered Joey and Bree, very much anticipating their wedding, now less than two weeks away.

My dad lifted his voice. "Are you going to be a model someday, Jess?"

She blushed with a giggle. Soon to be thirteen, Jess was tall for her age, as were all her siblings. She was beginning to adjust to her newer, older, more grown-up self with so much to look forward to.

Nikki, seventeen and in her senior year of high school, carefully opened a set of watches she had been hinting about. Mind you, they were not just any old watches, but had six colored bands to match different outfits. "Sweet! Thanks, Mom." Then she opened a book by Francine Rivers, her favorite author at the time, who was known for her historical romance novels.

Being a thinker, Nikki would typically be found sitting back, observing her surroundings while intently listening to the conversations around her. She was like her dad and seldom spoke before thinking things through. She opened a box with two pink sweaters inside. Pink was a color she had never worn before but had always wanted to try. She liked to try new things. Her sense of adventure called her to a different high school that offered a wider curriculum and extracurricular activities, with greater opportunity to make new friends. She was on the cusp of adulthood.

Krista dove into one of the largest packages under the tree. Her face lit up as she unwrapped a framed print of Van Gough's *Starry Night*, the same image she had painted on the wall outside of her art classroom at school. She wrote songs and poems and played and sang in a band with Joey and his friends. Recently, she had added photography and videography to her creative repertoire. She loved taking photos and videos with her new video camera.

The next gift Krista opened generated a lot of interest. It was a small book about fulfilling one's heart's desire by delighting in God.

Krista, age nineteen, made friends with people of all ages. She had a lighthearted and disarming way of drawing and inviting people of all sorts into a place of acceptance. She began to grasp more fully the godly influence she could spread by taking a stand for her convictions and the things God was showing her.

Finally, Joey and Bree opened their gifts. First, a bottle of suntan lotion as a tease for the next gift—a set of luggage to use on their fast-approaching honeymoon to Cancun.

The girls had had their hand in matchmaking by taking part in a coalition of friends to bring Joey and Bree together. This made it extra fun for Krista as she videotaped looks and gestures of affection between the two of them. Nikki looked up to Joey and Bree so much—all three sisters did. They felt honored and thrilled to be in the wedding. I could almost taste the excitement in the air.

Into the midst of all this romped Buddy, our little white furball of a dog, a Bichon Frise, which translates into "curly-haired lap dog." He was mainly Nikki and Jess's dog, but since Krista had been living on her own for a few months, he was happy to see her.

Christmas Eve singing around the piano

Joey and Bree after opening luggage for the honeymoon that was postponed for a year

Family photo – Christmas Eve 2003

"Here, Buddy!" Krista beckoned Buddy to play.

Jess countered, "No, Buddy, come by me!"

My mother motioned for him to come to her, but Buddy decided it was Bree he wanted. She had food on her plate. Buddy loved all the attention and cuddled with whomever would have him or bribe him with food.

Soon we left for Joe's sister's house for more food, fun, and presents.

Come Christmas morning, Jess bounded downstairs, the first one down. She plunged a hand into her Christmas stocking that hung by the fireplace. Krista followed suit, and by the time Joe and I arrived downstairs, their stockings were empty, with Krista eagerly videotaping the excitement. Soon after us came Mom and Dad, Nikki, and then Jenna, my niece who lived with us. Joey and Bree had already left for Renville, a two-hour drive away, to celebrate with her family.

My mom had always made Christmas a fun time as I was growing up, and I tried to carry out some of those same traditions in my own family. Stockings full of goodies was one of them. In two hours my older brother Mike and his family, and my sister Kathie and her family, would all be arriving for a dinner I had yet to prepare.

Krista and my dad sat at the piano and serenaded us with just about every Christmas carol that existed. Then the rest of the family arrived, arms and bags overflowing with presents and their assigned food dishes. The ham baking in the oven warmed the house and sent out a mouthwatering aroma for everyone who walked through the front door.

Jess, who was first chair in her school band, got out her clarinet and played along with the new accompaniment CD of Christmas carol jazz arrangements. Kathie, always eager to have fun, added to the entertainment along with my dad and mom, who showed off their dance steps as Jessica played.

After eating our fill, we made our way to the living room. Dad read a touching prayer for our soldiers serving in Iraq, and we prayed for

Nikki, Jess, and Krista with stockings on Christmas morning

Buddy on Christmas Day

Debbie's parents dancing to
Jessica's clarinet playing

Jess playing clarinet on Christmas Day

them and their families. I read a poem Krista had adapted from "'Twas the Night Before Christmas" called "'Twas the Week Before Christmas," which our church youth group had done for a skit the previous week. The night ended singing karaoke on Mom and Dad's new karaoke machine, and listening to Krista beat-box to "Jingle Bells."

The week between Christmas and New Year's Day flew by fast. Mom and Dad, Joe and I, and the kids all had our traditional Christmas brunch the day after Christmas at the apartment Joey and Bree had found earlier in the month. It was less than a mile from our house and would be their home after they were married. Joey was living there until Bree would join him after the wedding. She had lived with us for a month the previous summer while Joey lived on campus and worked downtown. The girls loved Bree, and she was already part of our family.

The rest of the week was taken up with last-minute wedding preparations, building up our ever-growing anticipation for the wedding itself. Krista and I made table favors, which meant we wrapped half a dozen mint-flavored Hershey kisses in tulle and attached a little note on each one that read, *Love Is in the Air – Joseph & Brienne Mayer – 1/3/04*. The girls and I also enjoyed making hospitality baskets to place in the hotel rooms for our out-of-town guests. We filled the baskets with bread, chocolate-covered pretzels, assorted fruit and nuts, coffee, and packets of hot chocolate.

This was our first wedding with potentially three more to go.

One night, Nikki and Jess recruited my parents to help make chocolate bars for the rehearsal dinner while I was at Minnesota Teen Challenge, a faith-based recovery treatment program where I worked two nights a week. I hated to miss anything happening at home but couldn't get time off.

When I arrived home at 11:30 p.m., I breathed in the tempting scent of the last pan of bars baking in the oven, then watched Nikki and Mom beat Dad and Jess at our favorite family card game.

We loved having Mom and Dad with us during such a special time. My parents never missed the kids' school concerts, plays, basketball games, and Sunday school programs. The kids treasured their grandparents. They loved to watch movies and play board games with my mom, and they enjoyed outdoor games, anything competitive to play, with my dad. But since the basketball court lay covered with snow, they settled for bumper pool in the basement.

New Year's Eve finally arrived with the rest of our out-of-town company. My younger brother David, his sweet wife, Christy, and their three young children arrived that day.

Krista and Nikki always looked forward to entertaining their younger cousins, and David's kids ate up the attention from their older cousins. Jessica enthusiastically welcomed them to camp out in her bedroom, specifically rearranged for the occasion. Patty, my older sister, her husband, Ken, and two of their adult children were the last ones to arrive.

The fun time of family reuniting had begun. The adults and younger cousins celebrated at Mike's house, while the older cousins caught up at the Hard Rock Cafe. The excitement escalated with the wedding just three days away.

Three days.

The whole family had come together, and we anticipated more celebrating to come. Who knew when or what our next family event would be?

Krista and Debbie's dad playing bumper pool

Debbie's parents playing "Hand & Foot" with Nikki and Jessica

Chapter 5

What Am I Going to Do?

You never know how much you really believe anything
until its truth or falsehood becomes a matter of life and death to you.

—*A Grief Observed* by C. S. Lewis

B ye, Mom!"
Bye, Nikki.

"See you later!"

Bye, Jessica.

"Bye, Mom!"

Bye, Krista.

After my hugs in the foyer, Joe went out in the snow and said the last goodbye. I had bridesmaid dresses to iron and things to pack. Then my three daughters drove off to meet Bree and the other bridesmaids at the Green Mill for dinner.

Joey picked up his best man at the airport and came by to greet us, then they hurried off to his apartment. My brother and his family, who were staying with us, went out to dinner.

The house was quiet.

As I ironed, I felt strange. Depressed. Tired. *Of course,* I thought, *who wouldn't be a little worn out after the holidays?*

It was more than that. My soul felt drained.

And anxious.

I tried to comfort myself. *At least everyone is having a wonderful time.*

We'd leave the next day for Willmar, where we'd have the biggest celebration of all. I began packing a few things while thinking the whole time, *My son is actually getting married the day after tomorrow. It's hard to let go, but that's life. Get used to it, Debbie. And think about how you're gaining a daughter.*

While I packed, I still felt uneasy. I didn't know why. "Joe, something is not right here," I told him. "Can we pray and commit things to God again?"

We did.

I called my sister Patty to make sure everyone had the right directions to the church and asked her to pray too.

Why am I like this tonight?

Eight p.m. The phone rang. It was Bree. "Have you heard from the girls? They called me around six and said they'd be here at the Green Mill in half an hour."

An hour and a half ago. It's taking them way too long to get there. They must have stopped for coffee and lost track of time. That's it.

We called their cell phones. First Krista's, then Nikki's. No answer.

My heart pounded. I called Patty for prayer again. *I will not give in to fear. Everything will be okay.* I felt shaky, with my nerves on alert, while I tried to fold clothes in the basement. Suddenly, I collapsed on the floor and cried out to God. Fear had overwhelmed me like a crushing wave, but somehow, in that moment, I knew God was with me.

The phone rang again. Joe answered. Bree again. "I was told there's been an accident. Involving three girls. They've been admitted to the hospital. A state trooper is coming to talk to me."

When Joe came to tell me, everything seemed to freeze. I may even have stopped breathing. Upstairs, Joe could get no information from the state highway patrol. He called the hospital in Willmar. As I reached the top of the stairs, I heard two words through the phone receiver: *medical examiner.*

I screamed.

Stunned, Joe sat at the table, the phone held close to his ear. "All three?"

My hand battered the table. "No!" I slipped into a daze, vision blurred, stumbling in circles. "What am I going to do? What am I going to do?" I flung open the patio door and dashed outside, barefoot and in my pajamas. I wanted to run away. Nowhere to go. I staggered aimlessly on the icy, snow-covered patio. "What am I going to do? What am I going to do?" I could find no other words.

As I stumbled back into the house, a deluge of emotions continued to sweep over me. Couldn't sit. Couldn't stand still. Didn't know what to do. Energy churned inside me. I paced the room like a caged animal.

My brain seemed to stop. I couldn't think. My chest tightened as if trying to keep my heart from exploding. This panic felt like being trapped under water and fighting for air, not knowing which end is up.

Overwhelmed.

Lost in a swell of emotions, I was oblivious to the trauma Joe was experiencing. Later, I learned he reined in his own emotions for fear he would make things harder for me. While I was falling apart, he rose to the responsibilities at hand and made phone calls.

He called my brother Mike's house, where Mom, Dad, and Patty's family were staying, and broke the devastating news to them. Patty screamed in anguish, and Mike put his fist through the hallway wall, leaving not one but three gaping holes—like the holes in our hearts for each of the girls.

I paced around in the house, reciting my grief-stricken mantra, "What am I going to do?" until my brother David's car pulled up in the driveway. He had felt inexplicably compelled to forego the movie they had intended to see, sensing they were to return to the house.

At the sight of his car, I burst out of the house in my pajamas and ran down the steps, wildly waving my hands in the air, stomping through the snow, and screaming hysterically, "They're gone! They're gone! They're all gone!"

I would not be able to say the "D" word for many months.

Christy opened the car door and let out a loud scream when she realized what my hysteria meant. She followed me back into the house while trying to comfort me. David trailed behind, struggling to take in what he'd just heard.

He saw Joe staring blankly at a wall in the family room and approached him to ask him for clarity. David knew Joe to be a steady man, but this was different. He appeared almost catatonic. His eerie calm was more unnerving to David than my emotional outbursts.

Joe slowly turned his head toward him. "The girls were in an accident. It's true. They all died." We have since learned that both of our reactions were normal. Joe would, in time, identify and express his raw emotions, but at that time, other tasks demanded his energy and attention.

David returned to his kids in the car and calmly explained to them, "You guys, there was an accident, and Krista, Nikki, and Jessica are all in heaven."

After a moment of silence, six-year-old Caleb responded with a smile, "So ... they're with Jesus."

Nine-year-old Jordan, however, quickly surmised the full meaning of what had been said, and her eyes widened as she cried out and began sobbing. Four-year-old Hannah, watching her big sister's reaction, also began to cry. Before David could say anything else, Caleb's smile was gone and he too was weeping. David's composure disappeared and tears streamed down his cheeks too. He climbed onto the van floor with his children, and they all cried and hugged as tightly as they could.

Inside the house, everything slipped into slow motion for me. Like I was half-awake from a nightmare, time was impossible to measure.

I could hear everything that was going on, but I was not consciously present. Everything faded to black and white. Adrenaline surged through my entire being, yet I felt like life had ceased to be real. I was outside looking in. Helpless. In despair, I said, "I will never sing again."

The police chaplain's car pulled up to our house, followed by Deb and Stew, close friends who had been our previous pastor and his wife. Traumatized, my body still surged with a torrent of chaotic energy. The police chaplain suggested I get dressed and take a walk. My friend Deb walked with me down the street that I had so often enjoyed walking or biking with Jessica. I felt cruelly empty and cold, swallowed in the dark winter night. Although the moon lit the night sky, I felt engulfed by cold darkness.

I must wake up! This all is a bad dream. Has to be. I had these kinds of nightmares before. The ones that seemed so real—when your words won't come out and your heart pounds from fear.

When Deb and I returned to the house, of course nothing had changed. My nightmare was still my reality, and I could not wake up from it. Ever.

Mike and Sandi, our current pastor and his wife, soon arrived, followed by Patty, Ken, and Mike.

Joey called from the Willmar hospital. "I love you, Mom."

It was so reassuring to hear his voice that I didn't want to hang up. "I love you too."

We later learned that when Bree heard the news of the accident, she had been told by a person from the hospital to stay at the restaurant until an officer could come to her there. When the trooper arrived, Bree asked him if the girls were all right. He simply stated, "No, they're all dead."

She cried uncontrollably, and waited about twenty minutes before she could bring herself to call Joey, who was on his way to Willmar with Jordan. When she called him, she tried to tell him what had happened but was too hysterical to speak clearly. Joey asked her to repeat her words three times before he could understand them. Fortunately, Jordan was driving. Sensing something was very wrong, Jordan grabbed Joey's hand and began to pray.

When Joey and Jordan arrived at the hospital, Bree was waiting for him there with her parents, the remaining bridesmaids, the pastor, and other members from their church.

After the initial shock, Joey and Bree felt strongly that the girls would want us to go ahead with the wedding. Joe and I agreed. All three pastors advised us to wait until morning to make our final decision.

Those of us at the house gathered in the living room to pray. We joined hands, and as I bowed my head, my eyes fixed on a single frame of three photos that sat on the bookshelf in front of me. Krista, Nikki, and Jessica—framed for posterity as a keepsake, their images stood side by side—as brides. I had taken the pictures years earlier when I was trying on my dress in preparation for a renewal of Joe's and my wedding vows. They'd taken turns trying it on to see themselves as brides, a girl's most romantic dream.

As my eyes gazed at the pictures, these words bubbled up within my heart and flowed out of my mouth: "They are now My beautiful brides, and I am their Bridegroom." As I spoke them, the Lord's words brought me peace and back to reality.

Photo of the girls as brides

47

Only a few months before, the girls and I had listened to a teaching tape about the bride of Christ and the intimate relationship God desires to have with us. The analogy of marriage represents the love of Christ for the church. In Ephesians 5:25–27, Scripture speaks of Jesus Christ, the Bridegroom, sacrificially and lovingly choosing the church, made up of individual believers, to be His bride.

In biblical times, the betrothal period was the time during which the bride and groom were separated until the wedding. In our present age, we who are the bride of Christ are also in that period of betrothal. As believers, we are His bride, waiting with great anticipation for the day we will be united with our Bridegroom. The full intimacy with Christ we so greatly long for will not happen until He returns. During our preparation time—which is now—we know Him but cannot see Him in His full glory.

There are a lot of things that are true, but only *the* truth will set us free, which is God's Word—the firm foundation of my life. It was certainly true that my daughters were in a car crash and had been killed. They were gone. But the larger, overshadowing truth is that they are alive to God, eternally His brides.

My comfort was, and still is, that my girls are the Lord's brides, completely loved, completely taken care of, and completely free. They are forever His, enjoying His intimate presence.

On this side of heaven, I would soon begin the struggle of walking out this loss in my humanity. For now, God carried me like a baby in His strong arms of love.

The sudden immensity of the tragedy had left me saying, "What am I going to do? What am I going to do?" I certainly did not know what to do. No one did at first, but I'm thankful we remembered who did, and called to Him in prayer, "We do not know what to do, but our eyes are on you" (2 Chronicles 20:12b).

⌒ Chapter 6 *⌒*

Tokens
From Heaven

*What we love about this life are the things that
resonate with the life we were made for.
The things we love are not merely the best this life has to offer—
they are previews of the greater life to come.*

—HEAVEN BY RANDY ALCORN

I was told how overwhelmed my mom was when she heard the news, but by the time she arrived, she was stronger—relying on the faith she consistently displayed while I grew up. My heart broke to see my dad weeping as he collapsed in the corner of our front hall. He kept repeating, "Why not me?"

Something in the unfolding moments gave me a glimpse of a much bigger story than just my own. I knew God would somehow use this unthinkable tragedy. In the midst of my breaking heart, I felt God calling me to something way beyond myself.

Amazed at my rising strength, I began to comfort the people around me. I had a sense that this life is short, explaining to several others that human life—compared to eternity—is like a quickly vanishing vapor. I was exceptionally conscious of the reality that this life is short—and eternity is forever (James 4:14).

Later that night we began pulling out pictures, scrapbooks, and school projects, sharing stories about the girls. God began to give us tokens of eternity to infuse us with hope in the midst of our over-whelming loss. One of these tokens was a senior art project Krista had made, describing herself in words and pictures.

On the first page, she introduced the project and expressed her relationship with God. Her older brother Joey, even as a toddler, had been sensitive to God. After watching a movie in kindergarten, he responded by praying a simple prayer with his teacher to know and follow Jesus for the rest of his life. He came home from school enthu-siastic and confident about his new commitment to God. In the fol-lowing days, preparing to be water baptized, he eagerly shared his experience with Krista and led her in a prayer as she invited Jesus into her heart as well. God had planted His seed of love in her young and tender heart, just as He had done in Joey's.

As I read the first page of her art project out loud, we learned that Krista's understanding of this love had matured along with a confi-dence of who she was as a Christian:

> Here's a book about me. I wish in words I could explain to you my true identity, but the definition of *identity* is "the condition of being one's self, and not another."
>
> I was born in the city. I grew up in South Minneapolis and I loved it! Every warm memory in my heart traces back to a little place I like to call home … the place where friends and family laid the foundation that formed me into the person I am today. At the age of three I knelt down next to my brother and with his help, made the most important and influential decision of my life. I asked Jesus Christ to come into my heart. Although at the time I didn't fully understand the impact of my humble little prayer, it has proven to be the most fruitful act I have ever made.
>
> Like all kids my age, I have my share of talents, many inter-ests, and hopes and dreams, but before I share them with you, it's important that you understand, "For me to live is Christ and to die is gain" (Philippians 1:21). Take away all material posses-

sions, all my talents and earthly desires, and I will be the same because of the life I have in Christ!

So now with that said, here's a little book about me …

It was as though she spoke directly to us in that moment: *Mom, Dad, don't be sad for us. We're good. We've gained everything!* "For me to live is Christ, to die is gain" is true.

We so often think of eternal life as something that happens after we die, and we put off thinking about it, but Jesus described eternal life as knowing Him—right now. "Now this is eternal life: that they know you, the only true God, and Jesus Christ, whom you have sent" (John 17:3).

Jesus tells us the very moment we put our faith in Jesus Christ, we gain eternal life that cannot be interrupted by physical death. "Very truly I tell you, whoever hears my word and believes him who sent me has eternal life and will not be judged but has crossed over from death to life" (John 5:24).

Shortly after the accident, a friend sent me a newsletter of John Piper's exposition on that verse, which opened my understanding:

> Already, by faith in Christ, our judgment is past, and our death is past. Death is no longer death for those who are in Christ. … Death is no longer the terror that it used to be. Death is now a transition from life to better life, from faith to seeing, from groaning to glory, from good fellowship with Jesus to far better fellowship with Jesus, from mixtures of pain and pleasure to all pleasure, and from struggles with sin to perfect affections for Jesus.[1]

Physical death does not separate us from true life; our sin does. Sin is living life our own way, apart from knowing and following God, who is the only source of eternal life. According to Scripture, there are plenty of people walking around this planet with blood pumping through their bodies—physically alive but spiritually dead. "For the wages of sin is death, but the gift of God is eternal life in Christ Jesus our Lord" (Romans 6:23).

It comforts me to know the girls' lives with God were not interrupted but continued on, and will go on for all eternity, just as 2 Corinthians 5:8 so clearly tells us: "We are confident, I say, and would prefer to be away from the body and at home with the Lord."

God wants to establish us now, in this present time, as eternal beings with eternal destinies.

While I eagerly paged through photo albums, grasping every memory I could, Joe was in the other room attending to phone calls. One was with the American Red Cross, which asked our permission for the donation of the girls' organs. Joe gave his consent as long as it was for life-giving purposes. He knew that hearing those words would have been too disturbing for me, so he spared me the added trauma.

Local newspapers also called, and again Joe assumed the responsibility of speaking for the two of us. A longtime friend of ours who had a ministry to India called to say he was leaving that night for India and that he would dig a water well and build a church in the girls' honor. That was just the beginning of an outpouring of comfort and support from the body of Christ that gave us so much consolation.

The night lingered on and brought more crying, comforting, hugging, and reminiscing.

At one point, I snuck away to Nikki's bedroom to breathe. I needed solitude for a few minutes. As I sat in the chair next to her bed, I longingly surveyed her room, hoping for some comfort. Some memories. Signs of her life that had been.

Through a veil of tears, my eyes scanned her bedroom walls plastered with a collage of photographs of her seventeen-year-old life. I desperately needed to pinpoint the familiar pictures to enter their memories. My aching heart had brief moments of reprieve as I stepped into the pictures, feeling her alive with me.

There we were in Jamaica, a New York City borough of Queens, on a youth mission's trip. I could feel the sun on my face and smell the Caribbean soul food. I recalled the excitement of asking people in public places if we could pray for them, which had ignited a new boldness in all of us. Nikki's face lit up whenever someone said yes.

A big smile found its way onto my face as I relived the time the four of us girls sat with Buddy, posing to mimic his crooked dog-smile. Searching frantically for pictures in which I could gaze into Nikki's gentle eyes lifted me to another place. But only briefly. Soon I was back, remembering where I was and what I was really doing.

While examining her room, I re-created the time we painted and wallpapered to match the down comforter she'd bought with her birthday money. We made curtains, a dust ruffle, matching pillow-cases, and a throw pillow for her bed. She especially had fun creating bubble letters for her name from leftover foil wrapping paper, which she artistically positioned above her window.

I picked up the red scarf and mittens from her desk. She loved scarves and hats, mix-matching them for different outfits. Tucking my hands inside the mittens, I snuggled them to my cheeks and smelled them as the fabric absorbed the wetness of my tears. Then I gently wrapped the scarf around my neck, sobbing some more, somehow hoping my cries would relieve the excruciating pain inside me.

After noticing her Bible on the desk, I picked it up and hugged it, then peeked inside, hoping to find something that revealed her heart. I found Matthew 6:19–21 highlighted: "Do not store up for yourselves treasures on earth, where moths and rust destroy, and where thieves break in and steal. But store up for yourselves treasures in heaven, where moths and rust do not destroy, and where thieves do not break in and steal. For where your treasure is, there your heart will be also."

Nikki was soft spoken and could easily be overlooked. She often reassured me by saying, "Don't worry, Mom. I'm okay." After reading this, it was as if I could hear her saying to me, "Mom, don't worry. We're okay. We have our treasure!" The next words I sensed her saying were: "You have to tell people there's so much more to living than just what this life has to offer."

I felt reaffirmed that my real life extends far beyond what I experience on this earth. Tasting salt from my streaming tears, I knew my girls would one day be as much a part of my future as they had ever been. This thought comforted me. I had three treasures awaiting me in heaven.

I felt as if I had just spoken with Nikki, knowing God had given me another one of His tokens from heaven, one more truth to wrap around my broken heart and calm my anxious thoughts. In spite of the many raw emotions raging through me, knowing the girls were with the Lord and that they were His brides brought me great peace in the midst of the broken pieces of my heart.

A little after 1:00 a.m., I suggested that people go home and try to sleep. Joe and I climbed into bed around 2:30 a.m.

It had only been a few hours since Nikki had modeled her new pink sweater, seeking the assurance that she looked as beautiful as she felt. I could still see Jessica as vividly as ever, clasping her new *The Lord of the Rings* book while walking out the door. And I could clearly hear Krista's voice, asking me in a little-girl tone—the one she teasingly used when she needed something—to iron the bridesmaid dresses and finish her laundry.

How can this be happening?

In a few short hours, we would wake up to face the daunting task of driving to the hospital in Willmar.

Hears a book about me. I wish in words I could explain to you my true identity, but the definition of identity is, "the condition of being one's self, and not another," so I guess the only way to achieve full understanding would be to be me. But maybe I can open up a little window, and let you peak inside.

I was born in the city. I grew up in South Mpls, and I loved it! Every warm memory in my heart traces back to a little place I like to call home. 3233 22nd Ave. So. Mpls, MN 55407 (my old address) is the place where friends and family laid the foundation that formed me into the person I am today. At the age of 2 I knelt down next to my brother and with his help, made the most important and influential decision of my life; I asked **Jesus Christ** to come into my heart. Although at the time I didn't fully understand the impact of my humble little prayer, it has proven to be the most fruitful act I have ever made.

Like all kids my age, I have my share of talents, many interests, and hopes and dreams, but before I share them with you, it is important that you understand, "For me to live is Christ, to die is gain," Philippians 1:21. Take away all material possessions, all my talents, and earthly desires and I will be the same because of the life I have in Christ!

So now with that said, here's a little about me...

Opening page of Krista's journal

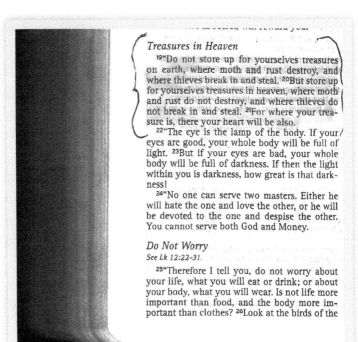

Treasures in Heaven

[19]"Do not store up for yourselves treasures on earth, where moth and rust destroy, and where thieves break in and steal. [20]But store up for yourselves treasures in heaven, where moth and rust do not destroy, and where thieves do not break in and steal. [21]For where your treasure is, there your heart will be also.

[22]"The eye is the lamp of the body. If your eyes are good, your whole body will be full of light. [23]But if your eyes are bad, your whole body will be full of darkness. If then the light within you is darkness, how great is that darkness!

[24]"No one can serve two masters. Either he will hate the one and love the other, or he will be devoted to the one and despise the other. You cannot serve both God and Money.

Do Not Worry
See Lk 12:22-31.

[25]"Therefore I tell you, do not worry about your life, what you will eat or drink; or about your body, what you will wear. Is not life more important than food, and the body more important than clothes? [26]Look at the birds of the

Nikki's Bible

Chapter 7

Beautiful Departure

Let us never forget that He walks with us on this side of the curtain.
And then guides us through the opening.
We will meet Him there, because we have met Him here.

—Erwin Lutzer

January 2, 5:30 a.m.
I crawled out of bed. Hadn't slept at all. The water spraying from the shower mixed with the tears pouring from my eyes. I wished the water could wash away my pain. Sweep it all away.

Joe's strong arms held me on his lap as we sat on the side of the bed. I felt safe there, not wanting to move. I wanted him to cradle me like a baby and tell me everything would be okay. But I knew his heart was as broken as mine. We cried out and asked God to send us people to help us through what seemed impossible.

Too soon, Patty and Ken were in one car, Stew and Deb in the next, and Joe and me in the last one. Our caravan of mourners set off for Willmar. Our first answer to prayer. Ken felt commissioned from God to support and protect Joe. Patty knew the minute she heard the news of the crash, she just had to be at my side. Deb and Stew had always been faithful and supportive friends, so it was no surprise when they came to help. However, these six were only the first of our band of hand-holders.

While peering out the car window at the dreary landscape, I felt detached from the world. Thoughts snuck in and overwhelmed me for all that needed to be done, but I also I sensed God's presence.

I focused on the list I had of things to do. First, find a funeral home. The police chaplain had recommended a couple in our area, so I called the closest one. The director spoke with kindness and compassion, reassuring me that he would contact Pastor Mike and take care of everything. What a relief. One thing crossed off the list.

Next, we had to write the obituary. I couldn't believe what we were doing, but describing our girls on paper brought us both comfort. Another thing crossed off the list. *Maybe if enough is crossed off the list, I'll feel better?*

Halfway there, we stopped for coffee. The other two couples acted uncomfortable while making a coordinated effort to stand in front of a newsstand to block our view of it.

At the hotel Joey was staying at, I got out of the car in a daze. We traded hugs and tears. A few feet away from us stood another newsstand. This time I saw the paper's front page—and on it a photo of the demolished car and the pink flower on Krista's dashboard twisted into a new pose. The image glared at me, taunted me, and stabbed me with horror.

I didn't want to see it, but a morbid curiosity drove my eyes to look. Nausea rose up and my head felt dizzy with pain. An arm embraced me from behind.

I'd never been much of a hugger, but after the news of the crash, I needed physical touch-from people who cared to stay present. Their compassion helped steady me as I stood at the edge of an emotional cliff. Without the touch from others, I would easily slip over the edge.

At the hospital, we braced ourselves for the daunting task of saying goodbye to the girls. Before we went in, my brother David, who had stayed back at our home in New Brighton, called to tell us that the media had been at our door all morning. We dictated a statement he could tell the reporters and gave him permission to use their school pictures and the photos of the girls each dressed in my wedding dress.

In the waiting room, Bree and her parents met us with more hugs and tears. We awkwardly discussed whether to proceed with or postpone the wedding. Joey, Bree, Joe, and I all knew we wanted to go on with the wedding, knowing the girls would want it that way. We agreed that they would be disappointed if we didn't. We just needed to convince the others. After some time, our group compassionately acquiesced to our wishes.

The time came to do the hardest thing I had ever done in my life.

We began the long, surreal walk down a sterile, white hallway. It felt like something out of a suspense film. I felt uneasy and apprehensive as I was about to walk into the most horrifying moments of my life. I wanted it to be over before it started, but I also longed to say goodbye to my daughters.

We stopped at an intimidating door that seemed as if it would open to the afterlife. Feeling shaky and threatened by what awaited me on the other side, I took a deep breath and stepped into the room.

There they were.

My three daughters. Lying on tables.

The room was small and dimly lit. No color. Just white sheets that draped their bodies, and their grayish-white faces and arms. Even the air was dead. *Will I pass out?*

Everything moved in slow motion. It was taking so long but had barely started. *Oh God, please help me!*

I saw Nikki first. Just one glance and my knees collapsed under me. I felt sick to my stomach. Deb's arm wrapped around mine and helped me to a chair. After gaining my equilibrium, I got up and stood beside Nikki's side again. My precious daughter. Not even twenty-four hours earlier, she'd modeled her new pink sweater. Being the one behind the wheel, she suffered the worst injuries. There she lay on the cold, hard table. Lifeless. Her jaw and nose broken, twisted, and disfigured. Never again would she wonder how she looked in pink. What lay in front of me didn't even look like her. I wanted to nudge her just enough for her to hear me say it would be all right, but I only stroked her highlighted hair and said, "I love you!"

Krista lay beside her. As a way of connecting one last time, I made myself touch her cold, scratched arm and face. Her face wasn't as injured as Nikki's but was equally as hard to touch and look at. My invincible Krista. The girl who broke her teeth twice while playing basketball in the church gym and, oblivious to her pain, kept playing. She had recently been the only girl to play on an all-men's basketball team. Not much could get her down or keep her down. I'm sure she tried to hold on, but death's grip overpowered hers. "You beat me to heaven," I cried, then told her, "I love you!"

When I came to Jessica, it was almost unbearable. My sweet, silly little girl who was leaving her childhood behind, becoming as good at basketball as her older sister Krista, lay lifeless on a table beside her. *How can this be? My baby. Still and breathless.* She looked peaceful, but she was gone. I painfully bent down and hugged her stiff body. Weeping, I kissed her cold face. Then I told her, "I love you!"

I couldn't bear another moment. I had to leave before I fainted or collapsed onto the floor. I felt dazed and weak. Drained of everything inside me. Run over by sorrow, as if a semi-truck had hit me on the same road.

Debbie and Patty followed me into another room. I sat. Stunned.

I watched as Ken and Stew stayed with Joe, who needed a while longer with his girls. His initial reaction upon seeing them deepened the shock he was already in. He was numb, unable to identify or express any of the emotions running wild inside him. He lingered a while—his way of expressing his love for the girls. Then he gently touched and kissed each of them for the last time.

He came out of the room and slowly managed to share something vital from his heart: "I noticed distinct smiles on both Krista and Jessica's faces." He paused and then said reassuringly, "And I could see the remains of a smile hidden under the injuries on Nikki's damaged face too."

I took his hand in mine. I had been too absorbed with my own sorrow to notice anything other than their lifelessness.

Those smiles brought him an awareness of the reality that they were not there in the bodies he saw lying on the tables. He knew they were alive in heaven with Jesus. I knew it too.

Later, Joe asked our friend Debbie, who was a nurse at Children's Hospital and frequently witnessed the death of patients, if a smile was a normal occurrence on the face of someone who dies. She said it was not—which confirmed to Joe that the girls' expressions were a response to seeing Jesus' face.

We learned that Nikki and Jess died at the scene, and Krista at the hospital. We would wait until later to piece together the details of how the accident happened. Some grief is so heavy that one can only carry it in portions, a little at a time.

We wouldn't hear until weeks later from Joey about his experience of identifying his sisters' bodies the night before we came. Not sure how he'd react, and not wanting to put Bree through more distress, he went in to see them with only a nurse. The girls had not yet been cleaned up from the accident and were in bad shape. After he'd gained his composure, he said to the hospital staff, "Please don't let my parents see them like this."

Being the big brother, he often prayed for his sisters, especially Jessica, since she was the youngest. He had frequently asked God to spare her from the evil in the world. He prayed that she would remain with the pure heart she so consistently displayed. When he saw her lying on the table, though her body was limp and lifeless, he saw no evidence of physical trauma. He told us that she had a peaceful smile that spoke to him of how God preserved her innocence even in her death. The pleasure on her face was a picture for Joey of Jessica beholding Jesus, and evidence of his prayers answered. A few years later he would write a song, "Beautiful Departure," that articulated his moving experience.

While I had been writing the song for Joey and Bree's wedding, the girls told me they all wanted me to sing in their weddings. I then realized that the funeral would be their weddings.

As I thought about how Nikki would often say, "Don't worry, I'm okay," I knew what I would sing at the funeral—"If You Could See Me Now," a song that speaks from the viewpoint of the departed, that their loved ones would not want them to come back if they could see their eternal happiness. I could clearly hear Nikki in my mind: "Don't worry about us, Mom. If you could see us now, and what we're experiencing, you would never want us to come back!"

After seeing the girls on those tables, I was so aware that they were not there. What made their personalities, spirits, and character so unique was clearly absent. Second Corinthians 5:8b describes it as "to be away from the body and at home with the Lord." I knew my girls were in the Lord's presence, safe with Him, enjoying Him.

Patty told me that when she saw them, she was reminded it was only their shells, their earthly "tents" lying on the tables. "For while we are in this tent, we groan and are burdened, because we do not wish to be unclothed but to be clothed instead with our heavenly dwelling, so that what is mortal may be swallowed up by life" (2 Corinthians 5:4).

Reflecting on that truth, I wanted Joey and Bree to sing "I Can Only Imagine" and the three of us to sing "I Hear Angels." Both songs depict the atmosphere and activity in heaven, where the saints and angels worship around the throne of God. I also knew I wanted to sing a song I had sung at my Grandma Nannie's funeral, "Softly and Tenderly," an invitation to know Jesus extended to those who remain. Reflecting on the truths of these songs gave me immense comfort. I strongly sensed that the girls liked them too.

After seeing the girls on those tables, lifeless to this world, I wondered if I could sleep that night. Those with us felt it wise for me to see a doctor before we left the hospital. He prescribed a very low dose of Ativan for me to use for the next couple of days as needed.

I'm so glad that God meets us in our humanity. He doesn't require us to be strong and perfect. He's strong and perfect. He just wants us to call out to Him and depend on Him. He meets us where we're at to bring us somewhere better. That better place for me would come after a long series of struggles and victories. That's why it's called a *journey* of faith. God loves us just the way we are and is faithful to help us in our need, loving us the way only He can, then He brings us into a greater place of truth and freedom.

We're all unique with different strengths and weaknesses. I discovered we cannot, and need not, compare ourselves or our stories to others. Our stories belong to us, and we're the only ones who can walk them out.

Chapter 8

Carried

God gives unusual strength
when unusual trials come upon us.
—Charles Spurgeon

Crazy as it sounds, after saying goodbye to our girls at the hospital, Deb and Stew joined Joe and me at the legion hall to prepare for the rehearsal dinner that same evening. Since we decided to go ahead with the wedding, we had preparations to carry out. The rest of our group left to decorate the church sanctuary for the wedding itself. Despite our broken states, we all determined to make the wedding as positive for Joey and Bree as possible.

I know what we did was an unusual way to channel emotional energy after someone dies, especially when three of your children died at once, but this New Year's Day of 2004 marked a new definition of *unusual* for me. God's supernatural strength gave me unusual ability to do the unusual. I would describe the next couple days more like being carried than walking, and in the following days, weeks, and months, I would find myself doing many more unusual things as well.

As we each carried out our surprisingly therapeutic tasks, Joe said he could almost feel the presence of our daughters. They loved to have fun and celebrate. It was as if they were smiling when everyone enjoyed the preparations, and gently scolding us when anyone became engrossed in grief. At least for the next couple of days, we just couldn't grieve. We had a wedding to celebrate.

On our way back to the church, we received a call informing us that reporters were waiting there to interview us. When we arrived, we were surprised to find an entire press conference ready and waiting for us. Reporters from four major television stations filled the lobby with cameras and microphones. We prayed with Pastor Keith from the Willmar church and then proceeded to answer the reporters' questions. I was honored to talk about my girls and my God. I was so aware that it was beyond me that I wasn't nervous.

Every station that aired our story spoke openly about our faith in God and our hope of heaven. God used the news media as a tool in His hand to reveal Himself to surrounding communities through us, just ordinary people who desperately needed Him.

"I have three girls that would possibly get married one day," I said, "but God showed me that they are now His brides. He's the Bridegroom, and they are with Him right now, and they are beautiful brides. God is going to use this because He always brings something good out of bad. It doesn't mean we're not hurting. But we know we'll see them again one day, and that makes it a little more bearable." They didn't edit out one single line.

We had no idea the news of the accident would spread throughout the entire country. We later learned that it was covered nationally and internationally on both CNN and the Associated Press World News. These newscasts pointed people to Christ, bringing Him honor and glory, and initiated an outpouring of prayer and support for us from people around the world.

The rehearsal dinner carried a strange sense of joy. Not happiness, but a peace and love flooded our hearts. I felt so much love for Joey.

I knew the girls would want us to celebrate Joey and Bree, and I was determined to make it a good time for them. Somehow I mustered the courage to do a silly impersonation of Joey as a pre-teen singing a song by Carmen, as he often did while singing along to a cassette tape. That was not something I would have naturally done, but so much of me had died that I wasn't concerned with what people thought of me. It was actually quite liberating. I only cared about blessing Joey and Bree, and wanted people to have a good time and not feel sad for us. I knew sorrow would come, but not that night. I think it was God's way of helping us deal with our shock.

We concentrated that night and the following days on enjoying the son we still had, endeavoring not to focus on the pain of the daughters we lost.

Later at the hotel, we watched my brother David and niece Jenna on the news. As my girls' faces appeared on the screen, David's voice confidently declared, "The girls not only believed, but lived their faith and are now with their beloved Bridegroom." One reporter spoke of the girls as an artist (Krista), a scholar (Nikki), and a budding musician (Jessica), sharing their mutual faith. As we watched an interview of a group of our daughters' friends and the school principal, we heard them all praise the girls' character and love for people. My girls were certainly not perfect, but they loved God and people, and I felt honored they were my daughters.

My heart ached when I saw my niece, in spite of her own shattered heart (they were her best friends), declare that God's plans were bigger than this accident. The news also quoted Pastor Keith saying, "We will watch and see God bring beauty from ashes."

It was bizarre to turn on the TV and see our names and our girls' faces on every news channel. We were astonished to see God telling His big story through our smaller one, once again realizing this was bigger than us. It seemed to be igniting extreme compassion throughout the entire upper Midwest. We knew countless prayers were being said on our behalf, and we felt remarkably strengthened by them.

That night as I lay in bed, disturbed by the memory of the image of their demolished car, I cried out to God. Haunted by tormenting thoughts and images of what they might have experienced, the Lord assured me that my perspective was limited. From this side of eternity, it was a terrible car crash. But from heaven's side, it was a beautiful homecoming. He reminded me to look at the eternal, not the temporal. He helped me to see that any horror the girls may have experienced during the crash was forgotten the instant they saw Him face-to-face.

Again, this truth brought peace to my heart.

How will God carry us through the wedding the next day? I wondered and then fell asleep.

Krista Mayer   **Nikki Mayer**   **Jessica Mayer**

Loved ones cope with deaths of 3 sisters

Newspaper headline,
Friday, Jan. 2, 2004

Image on TV news, Friday, Jan. 2, 2004

Debbie's brother David telling the media that Joe, Debbie, Joey, and Bree are confident the girls would not want wedding canceled

Niece Jenna telling news cameras God has a bigger plan than what we can see

TV news captured Joe and Joey full of sorrow

Debbie telling news reporters that her daughters are now brides in heaven

Newspaper captures friends Deb and Stew, and sister Patty comforting Debbie at the church before press conference

Chapter 9

Through Heaven's Eyes

They that love beyond the world cannot be separated by it.
Death cannot kill what never dies.

—William Penn

January 3, the wedding day. I climbed out of bed and stumbled into the shower. I leaned heavily against the shower wall and sobbed. I cried only one other time that day.

Before the wedding, I entered the room where Bree and the bridesmaids were getting ready. *This is not the way it's supposed to be.* I should be hearing Krista and Bree goofing off, as Krista would be painting Bree's nails and Jessica giggling while admiring her own. Nikki would be fixing her hair, so pretty with the new highlights that Joe had teasingly said made her look like a movie star.

The quiet atmosphere only accentuated the girls' absence. I wondered how Bree felt. Remembering the joy of my own wedding day, I wanted to be happy on her big day, but it was painful to be in this room. I managed a smile and a couple of photos, then gave her a hug and left to find a private place to cry.

After composing myself, I wandered down the hallway to see if I could sneak a peek at Joey. I found him and his groomsmen praying, huddled in a circle. For a moment, I flashed back in time. What I saw was a mirror image of my bridesmaids and me on my own wedding day. What a gift. It gave me the strength I needed to go forward. I thanked God, gave Joey a hug and kiss, and then headed to the lobby to greet wedding guests.

The lobby served as a place for our guests to show their own grief as well as love. Once again, we received warm hugs and kind sympathies, but not without tears.

Upon walking into the sanctuary, the atmosphere magically transformed into one of celebration. We credit that not only to our friends' support, but also to Pastor Keith's welcome and prayer before the ceremony. He essentially gave everyone permission to celebrate. After he walked in, he announced, "Given the circumstances surrounding today, we thought it would be a good idea to make sure we're all on the same page. Both the Mayer and the O'Connor families desire that today not be a day of sympathy, but a day of celebration. Today is the day we want to show reverence to the Lord Jesus Christ through the wedding of Joey and Bree. We want to create for them a memory they can treasure forever. So will you agree with me that this is going to be a celebration that grabs the attention of everyone in heaven?"

And a beautiful wedding it was.

Joey had written the music for the instrumental processional and titled it "Love Is in the Air." As the beautiful music played, Joey made his entrance, and my heart momentarily sank, knowing his three sisters would not come down the aisle. With butterflies in my stomach, I hoped to remain composed, knowing if I started to cry, the floodgates would let loose a torrent. To my surprise, as I observed Joey's countenance, I saw things from a different perspective.

Confirming Joey's song, love—supernatural love—truly was in the air. Joey miraculously beamed from ear to ear. He became even more radiant as he gazed at his lovely bride making her way down the aisle. I couldn't help but think of how Jesus is with each one of us who says yes to His invitation of love and eternal life with Him. As Joey's eyes shone with tender anticipation at the sight of Bree's entrance, I envisioned Jesus' eyes welcoming my girls as they walked down a heavenly aisle. "As a bridegroom rejoices over his bride, so will your God rejoice over you" (Isaiah 62:5b).

Joe and Debbie being greeted with
hugs and sympathies before wedding

Joey and his groomsmen praying
in hallway before wedding

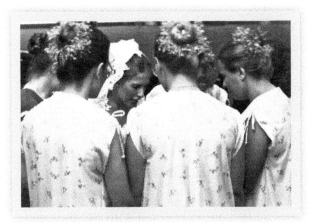

Debbie and bridesmaids praying
(in same pose) twenty-four years
earlier at her wedding

With my eyes stayed on Joey, I reflected on the sacrifices he had made in the last year for Bree. He had given up family vacation with us and had taken a semester off school to prepare financially for his wedding. He sacrificed, but he did it with joy and excitement. Jesus, our heavenly Bridegroom, also paid a price for us, anticipating the day He greets each of us at an altar in heaven: "For the joy set before him he endured the cross, scorning its shame" (Hebrews 12:2b).

Jesus' priceless sacrifice, however, was beyond what any human could emulate. His life's blood paid for our sins. "For you know that it was not with perishable things such as silver or gold that you were redeemed from the empty way of life handed down to you from your ancestors, but with the precious blood of Christ," as 1 Peter 1:18–19 tells us. Jesus desires to change us from sinners, stained with our own iniquity, into beautiful, radiant brides. As we receive Him now, we enter our time of "betrothal" and preparation while we await Him here on the earth.

Bree stepped gracefully down the aisle with equal anticipation, excitement, and love shining from her eyes—eyes for Joey alone. She was a beautiful, radiant bride. Nothing could have distracted her from her bridegroom in those moments. She knew how much Joey loved her, and he knew she loved him. This was a picture of the bride of Christ, knowing how much God loves each one of us. No distractions, as if "[looking away from all that will distract us and] focusing our eyes on Jesus, who is the Author and Perfecter of faith" (Hebrews 12:2a AMP).

Bree had spent the previous year preparing for this day, anticipating spending the rest of her life with Joey. It was such a clear picture to me of how we, as the bride of Christ, prepare for our heavenly Bridegroom, knowing that absolutely nothing can separate us from His love. It struck me to think that as we celebrated this wedding of Joey and Bree, there was a similar celebration taking place in heaven.

Although the wedding feast and marriage supper of the Lamb are still yet to come, David wrote in Psalm 16:11 that we have significant reason to celebrate and experience God's presence even now: "You make known to me the path of life; you will fill me with joy in your presence, with eternal pleasures at your right hand." If we on earth can experience joy in the presence of God, whom we do not see, how much more glorious will our joy be when we see Him face-to-face for all eternity?

Shortly after the wedding, we received a poem titled "Dual Weddings" from someone who had attended Joe's and my wedding twenty-four years earlier. The poem's author captured the eternal bridal theme beautifully.

DUAL WEDDINGS
by Reverend Jean Halvorson

Dual weddings did occur in Willmar sometime near New Year's Day
One prepared by human hands. The other far away.
Years ago, the mother of the groom sang for her wedding day;
She sang a four-part harmony of love that led the way.
Today, a long, white carpet announced the bride,
as she appeared in white,
While thoughts escaped to three young lives,
announced in Heaven that night.
Now three daughters left the earth, who harmonized in song,
Will be like doves on this great day that new life still belongs!
At this earthen altar, a bridegroom saw His bride
coming down the aisle,
Knowing the heavenly Bridegroom met his sisters with a smile!
Both weddings show the God of Love, though one is veiled in pain,
But pureness of the bridal scene reminds HOPE springs again.
Though on their way to stand as bridesmaids,
watching love in bloom,
Three jewels swept up to God's strong arms,
in Christ's own Bridal Room!

We didn't seriously think about canceling the wedding. But looking back, if we had canceled it, I don't know how any of us could have coped. In retrospect, we can see the wisdom of a loving God who encircled us with people who loved and cared for us. Ahead of us would be days and months, even years, to grieve. But for now we were enveloped by love, support, and warm bodies.

We requested that the wedding remain a private celebration (no TV cameras), but reporters stood outside the church. Some family and friends were interviewed at an off-site location and spoke about the wedding on our behalf. As we watched the news that night, it was staggering once again to see how God used our tragic event to declare the gospel of Christ. Through the internet as well, the compelling language of the kingdom of Love was openly broadcast across the state of Minnesota and far beyond. It stirred the hearts of people who already knew God to pray. For others, it aroused questions as to why God would allow such tragedy, which presented an invitation to learn more about God through our story.

Hebrews 12:27 says that God will shake what can be shaken, so that what cannot be shaken (His kingdom) will remain. In other words, when our lives are shaken and fall apart, it is God's intention that what is from Him is all that remains because being in Christ is unshakable.

True peace cannot be fabricated or conjured. It manifests from within the soul that abides in Christ and Christ in the soul—this process unfolds and matures with time through authentic relationship with Him.

A friend who attended the wedding said she didn't know how I was able to handle all that was happening. My response was, "I am finding that everything I have believed and taught my kids about God and His Word is true." And unshakable!

C. S. Lewis commented on this in *A Grief Observed:*

You never know how much you really believe anything until its truth or falsehood becomes a matter of life and death to you. It

Joey anticipating his bride

Bree meeting her bridegroom

Mr. and Mrs. Joseph Mayer

The family

is easy to say you believe a rope to be strong and sound as long as you are merely using it to cord a box. But suppose you had to hang by that rope over a precipice. Wouldn't you then first discover how much you really trusted it?[2]

I have learned that when our view is limited to this life only, many things make no sense. I know that as I have allowed the Word of God and the Holy Spirit to give me an eternal perspective, I have been able to trust in God's bigger plans and purposes. When I reach heaven and experience unspeakable joy, I will understand how the apostle Paul could speak of earthly suffering as light affliction:

> Therefore we do not lose heart. Though outwardly we are wasting away, yet inwardly we are being renewed day by day. For our light and momentary troubles are achieving for us an eternal glory that far outweighs them all. So we fix our eyes not on what is seen, but on what is unseen, since what is seen is temporary, but what is unseen is eternal. (2 Corinthians 4:16–18)

From a human perspective, my suffering was certainly not light. But Paul encourages us to look at unseen realties because one day our faith will become sight. When our mortal life ends, we will live by sight and no longer need faith because we will see Him face-to-face.

Scripture says we will see Him then, but God gives us glimpses now. He brings heaven to earth at special moments in the space that we call *time* as we choose to look to Him. The wedding was one of those times, and in a few days we would to see another glimpse of time and eternity meeting.

~ Chapter 10 ~

Almost There

*We see His smile of love even when others see nothing but
the black hand of Death smiting our best beloved.*
—CHARLES SPURGEON

How could something like this happen? This is a question every person at some point asks. Unfortunately—or maybe fortunately—Joe and I will never know exactly what happened between the time the girls pulled out of our driveway and collided with another car.

After many sleepless nights of wondering, I've come to the realization that by the time I reach heaven, and the answers, I will no longer need to know. But given the evidence from the state patrolman, the testimony of the other driver, and Bree's phone conversation with Nikki, I will attempt to describe my interpretation of what may have happened.

After saying goodbye and giving Joe and me a hug, Krista headed toward the front passenger side of the car. "Nikki, I don't feel like driving. Do you want to?"

"Sure."

"Thanks. I just want to sit back and listen to music."

The girls then set out for the Green Mill in Willmar, driving "Thumper," Krista's Dodge Lancer.

Jess anticipated reading her new *The Lord of the Rings* book in the back seat. "I like that music, but can you turn it down a little?"

"Okay, babe." Krista adjusted the volume, the driver's seat, and her long legs for the two-hour ride.

"I can't wait to get there. I'm hungry," Nikki said. Thinking about the wedding, she asked, "Hey, do you remember what Bree said they're serving at the reception?"

"No, I just remember they're having carrot cake," Krista answered. "You know that's what Mom and Dad had at their wedding."

"Carrot cake? Sweet!" Nikki remarked.

"Yum! That really sounds good," Jess said from behind her book. "Makes me hungry!"

Krista and Nikki sang along with the music—Nikki on melody and Krista on harmony. Jessica usually joined in the singing of that Sara Groves song, but she was busy enjoying her book.

As darkness fell, Jess put down her book. "Are we almost there?"

Krista perked up after her little rest and was ready to be silly with Jess now that she'd abandoned her reading. "Yeah, are we almost there, Mommy?"

Realizing they were running a little late, Nikki called Bree's cell phone. "Hi, Bree. Just wanted you to know we're about thirty minutes away. I'm so excited to see you!"

As usual, Krista mimicked in a goofy voice everything Nikki said.

"I'm tired and it's a little foggy. I can't wait to get there."

"We'll wait for you," came Bree's voice from the other end.

"Okay. See you soon." Nikki set her phone down.

As Nikki drove through the veil of fog, the headlights shined against the endless gray curtain.

Krista sighed. "Why does this seem like such a long way?"

"Yeah, I can't wait to get there," Jessica said.

"We're almost there," Nikki reassured herself and them. Her new watch read 6:30.

Only one mile from their destination.

The highway curved to the right, and they caught up to a car moving slowly in front of them. They were in a legal passing zone, and the lane on their left was open. But while they were passing the slower car, their lane began to narrow. They had to move over but couldn't.

"Nikki! Watch out!" Krista screamed.

Nikki tightened her grip on the wheel. Headlights were coming straight at them. She turned the steering wheel sharply to the right, trying to make it back into their lane. The tires screeched burning skid marks onto the road.

But it was too late.

"Watch out!" Jessica screamed and pulled her blanket over her head. She couldn't look.

In a flash of a second—impact! It was like the whole world exploded.

The Dodge Lancer struck a Plymouth Voyager minivan head on, and the girls' car spun off the road. Nikki's side of the car caved in so badly that it enveloped her. Krista and Jessica catapulted into the blast with bone-crushing intensity.

The next second all was still, all was quiet.

A Minnesota state patrolman reported that he had just completed investigating an accident when a call came in to respond to another accident farther down the highway at the passing lane, about a half a mile away.

While approaching the scene of the accident, he observed smoke and debris, and immediately knew the collision was a bad one. The left side of the car was too smashed in to free the driver, so he reached through the broken window of the passenger's side. The girl had no pulse, but her arm moved slightly. While examining her, another man arrived at the scene and, while offering to help, pointed to another passenger in the back seat, covered by a blanket.

The medical examiner concluded that both Nikki and Jessica died instantly—Krista, soon after. At the hospital, the doctor discovered that

Krista's aorta had been severed by the impact. I believe that the three of them saw Jesus together.

At the Green Mill, there was no sign of the girls. Bree called Krista's cell phone, then Nikki's. Neither of them answered. Bree wondered. Then she grew concerned.

She tried again. Still no answer.

She sat by the restaurant window, staring blankly out at the dark road—her eyes searching and then following each set of oncoming headlights. She willed the silver Dodge Lancer to come into sight—or at least she tried. All she got were two ambulances speeding past. Their screaming sirens nauseated her.

One of Bree's friends called the highway patrol to find out if there had been an accident involving three girls. Bree thought she might vomit. After no clear information from that call, her friend tried the hospital. Yes, three girls had just been admitted. Someone on the hospital staff said they were sending an officer to talk with Bree.

When the officer arrived, Bree sat in an almost catatonic state of shock.

He sat down. "What are the girls' names? How old are they? Where do they live?"

Bree felt completely numb. She could only grope for the simplest answers. She managed to quietly ask, "Can you tell me if they're okay?"

The officer said sadly, "I don't have the authority to give you any details because you're not family."

Not family. That stung. *Give us one more day and we will be.*

His final words hung in the air as he said them through his own distress: "They're all dead."

The driver of the minivan, a fifteen-year-old girl with a driving permit, suffered a fractured ankle. The other two passengers had no physical injuries. Her mother sat in the passenger seat, while her twelve-year-old brother sat in the back.

We knew the accident wasn't her fault. We also realized the young girl would be traumatized and feel guilty. Our hearts ached for her. We wanted to talk with her, but had no idea how to go about it, and so we prayed and asked God to help us.

Before the wedding started, a man stopped at the church and identified himself as the girl's father and a fellow believer. We embraced and cried together. He asked us if we would be willing to talk with his daughter before we left town. It was a quick answer to prayer.

The following morning on our way home, we stopped to visit her and her family. We cried with her, prayed for her, and told her it was not her fault, that she couldn't have avoided what happened. We affirmed that she had done all she possibly could have done.

We told her that we believed God was present at the scene of the accident. He could have prevented it, but He didn't. In His sovereignty, He brought my three daughters home while sparing her and her family. We told her we believed that God had plans for her and her family to be lived out together on this earth, and into eternity, just as He had plans for my girls and our family that extends into eternity. A car accident does not limit God's eternal purposes.

Then we all prayed together.

As we were leaving, her little brother, with tender, tearful eyes, approached us. He held out his hand. In it was a photo of the girls that he had picked up off the ground near the car. It was one of the girls that Krista had pinned to her visor. He timidly said, "I thought you might want this."

Chapter 11

Three Brides In Heaven

When we've been here ten thousand years bright shining as the sun;
We've no less days to sing God's praise than when we've first begun.

—JOHN NEWTON

Monday, January 7, two days after the wedding, our house was full of people from morning until night. We had a funeral to plan.

Friends and family busily made picture boards of the girls, reminiscing memories with smiles and tears. My nephews worked on creating bookmarks that would be inserted into the service programs. Friends and neighbors stopped by with care baskets to sustain us physically and emotionally. People and love surrounded us.

That evening, we met with the three pastors who would perform the funeral for our three daughters two days later. It felt so complete having both our former and present pastors with us, along with our brother-in-law.

Tuesday morning came quickly. When we arrived at the church for the visitation, a vast display of picture boards lined the perimeter of the sanctuary. These were made by friends of the girls from church and both the junior and senior high schools—alongside the ones already made at our house.

Joe, Joey, Bree, and I had time alone with the girls before the doors were opened. In their hands, they held baby's breath and red rose blossoms. They looked so beautiful in the bridesmaid dresses and the necklaces they would have worn for the wedding. This was the last time we'd see the earthly tents of our daughters. Gazing at their empty shells, I once again grew profoundly aware they were not there. Death had claimed only their bodies.

In a strange sense, this experience was extravagantly beautiful. An abundance of flowers displayed God's glory and the outpouring of love of their givers. A heavenly fragrance from the bouquets filled the sanctuary. The smell permeated the air reminding me of the joining of heaven and earth.

The joining of heaven and earth. This became our prayer: *Let Your kingdom come, to earth as it is in heaven.*

I believe one of the major reasons we witnessed such a palpable visitation from heaven was because the body of Christ set any differences aside and came together with one common purpose. Love. People from all over were either reaching out for love or extending it. Love comes from God, and so in loving one another, we were loving God Himself.

A string of people wrapped around the inside perimeter of the sanctuary for hours while looking at pictures as they waited to greet us and say goodbye to the girls. I believe many of them were looking for comfort, eager to experience God's faithfulness.

Toward the end of the night, everyone was seated so we could address them together. There were so many people, we couldn't possibly talk with each person. After standing for nearly six hours, we felt exhausted physically, but the overwhelming love and support from so many people energized us in spirit.

By Wednesday morning, my autopilot took over. Convinced that God was carrying us in His arms, we left for the funeral. God had undeniably displayed His glory and brought heaven to earth the day before.

Our church family from Vine Church, where we had been members for twenty years and where the kids grew up, contributed much to the service through music and testimonies. Our church family from Redeeming Love, where we had only been members for four months, offered their help by serving our needs before, during, and after the service, showering us with support. It really seemed that there was one church that day, as so many came together.

Joey, Bree, and I opened the service singing "I Hear Angels," which portrays worship in heaven. I knew the girls, and heaven itself, joined us in worship.

When our song ended, Pastor Mike said, "This is a service of celebration of eternal life. Three young sisters went home to be with their Lord and Bridegroom. And right now, even at this moment, Krista, Nikki, and Jessica are in the presence of Jesus Christ. They are three young ladies who had a love and a passion for Jesus, and He is their Bridegroom. They, along with all of us who look for His appearing, are His brides."

Although our emotions felt raw, the presence of the Lord Jesus Christ was stronger.

With a trembling voice, Joe led us in a heartfelt prayer, and the choirs from both St. Anthony and Irondale High Schools joined together and sang a song about believing in God through our pain. This song invited everyone—an estimated over two thousand people present—to look to God and believe, even if the tragedy made no sense to them. When I saw how the girls' deaths united so many people in love, I felt overwhelmed by God's love through them.

We heard a flood of memories expressed with heart-wrenching emotions through the eulogies of friends and cousins. A resonating theme was that all three girls cared about people and were greatly loved for who they were. One friend who knew the girls since infancy spoke through her sobs with wisdom beyond her years: "I've learned that the quality of someone's life can't be measured by how many years they've lived, but by how many lives they touched." As sad and heartbroken as I felt, I was encouraged to see God's love displayed through the lives of my girls.

When Joey and Bree sang "I Can Only Imagine," the music captured the hearts of everyone, reflecting what worship might be like in heaven. We allowed a major television station to televise the funeral, so there was news coverage throughout the day. We were amazed that segments of the message about our longing for heaven were broadcast on television news over the next few days. A common statement by all the stations reported that "faith in Christ" wove itself throughout a funeral that celebrated the girls' "eternal" lives.

Friends from Vine Church led us in worship with "Great Is Thy Faithfulness," a favorite family hymn. We were especially moved when a group of Jessica's friends from Vine sang a song that Jessica had introduced them to. I know that as these girls offered up their praise, Jess offered hers directly to Jesus in heaven. I believe the veil between heaven and earth is and was quite thin during the singing at that time.

As we love and worship God here and now, in the unique way we each do, we make ourselves ready for our place in eternity. C. S. Lewis puts it this way in *The Problem of Pain*:

> Surely each of the redeemed shall forever know and praise some one aspect of the Divine Beauty better than any other creature can. Why else were individuals created, but that God, loving all infinitely, should love each differently? If we all experienced God in the same way and returned Him an identical worship, the song of the church triumphant would have no symphony, it would be like an orchestra in which all the instruments played the same note. Heaven is a city, and a body, because the blessed remain eternally different: a society, because each has something to tell all the others—fresh and ever fresh news of the "My God" whom each finds in Him and whom all praise as "Our God."[3]

Lewis calls this the "secret signature of the soul."

Pastor Stew approached the mic next. "At this time, we all have questions and emotions, and yet I look at Joe, Deb, and the family, and I see lives that have been graced with strength and peace in spite of much sorrow," he said. "Without the hope that is anchored in the

Word of God, we have nothing. I know my own words cannot bring life, but God's words can, and that's what's sustaining you. Heaven and hope. I look at you both, having known you since 1978, and I think of this Scripture: Matthew 7:24–25, 'Therefore everyone who hears these words of mine and puts them into practice is like a wise man who built his house on the rock. The rain came down, the streams rose, and the winds blew and beat against that house; yet it did not fall, because it had its foundation on the rock.' Your house did not, and will not, fall because you have built it on Jesus, the Rock."

As I sang my adaption of "If You Could Only See Me Now," by Paul S. Morton, I could almost hear my girls saying to each other, "Don't you just wish they could see us now, so they wouldn't worry, so they'd know we're okay?"

"This is holy ground," declared my brother-in-law Ken when he took the microphone. "We've been celebrating three beautiful girls. We've laughed, we've cried, and we've heard many words and seen pictures that give us glimpses into their lives. But all these would just be words unless they held within them the promise of hope and eternal life."

He read the opening page of Krista's art journal: "Like all kids my age, I have my share of talents, many interests, and hopes and dreams. But before I share them with you, it is important that you understand, 'For to me, to live is Christ and to die is gain' (Philippians 1:21). Take away all material possessions, all my talents, and earthly desires, and I will be the same because of the life I have in Christ."

He proceeded with the question, "What does it mean, 'For me to live is Christ?' If I am living my life daily from an eternal perspective, I won't allow the things of every day to sweep over me, whether they be good or sad, and look back on my life and say, 'Where have the years gone?' One writer said of this Scripture that if you take Christ out of the statement and put anything else in there, it makes no sense. The equation is off, because all those things cease."

We inserted the bookmarks my nephews made into the funeral programs. They featured a picture of the girls with the Philippians 1:21 verse, including a "blank" line to fill in. It read, "For me to live is

THREE BRIDES IN HEAVEN

_____, to die is gain." Ken had explained that the bookmark was not only to remember the girls by but to have something tangible in the days, weeks, and months ahead to look at and consider the following questions: *What have I placed in the blank? For me to live is what? What is my life being spent for?* We can ask ourselves, *What am I doing, and why am I doing it?* We don't just need God when we leave this life; Jesus has come that we would have life and have it more abundantly—now.

Ken challenged each person not to leave until they confronted the blank in the Scripture, because nothing else will satisfy until Christ takes the central place on the bookmark of our hearts. Once Christ is central, we will have peace and joy that can never be taken away.

I sat staring at the three caskets, aware of the unalterable truth that this life is short and can end any minute. When Ken stepped away from the mic, silence filled the place. The Holy Spirit stirred hearts and called many to Himself. I realized God orchestrated the entire service, weaving in place each specific part as if we'd spent months preparing for it.

I sensed God's arms of love open wide to each person there while I sang the lyrics of the next song: "Softly and tenderly, Jesus is calling. Calling for you and for me."

Pastor Mike gave an invitation for those who didn't know Jesus to receive Him as their Savior. Streams of young people made their way to the front of the room, choosing to follow Jesus. About two hundred kids—students, friends, and family—made their way to the altar. About thirty adults raised their hands as well, responding to the Holy Spirit's invitation. Those were just the ones who physically responded. I don't think we will ever know the extent and impact the service had on the lives and hearts of people until we get to heaven.

Before we left for the cemetery, we stood in the church foyer with family and friends surrounding the girls' caskets. Pastor Mike asked, "Who gives these girls to their heavenly Bridegroom?"

Joe gently grasped my hand and said with assurance, "Their mother and I."

I squeezed his hand, and we both moved away from the caskets and proceeded outside to our cars.

In order to avoid traffic, the funeral procession wound along back roads that bordered parks and lakes on our way to the cemetery which overlooked the city. Everything looked so beautiful. Peace and well-being flooded my soul, even while acknowledging what kind of vehicle I was riding in, why I was riding in it, and where I was going. I felt deep loss for my girls, but at the same time, strong awareness of God holding me.

On this cold winter's day, the silvery afternoon sun shone on the girls' caskets next to three side-by-side plots. A heavenly kind of beauty surrounded us as we sang the first verse of "Amazing Grace." God's grace poured out on all of us. Even when walking away from the caskets, knowing they would be lowered into the cold ground, I was at peace because I knew where their spirits were and that they were more alive than ever.

We bury bodies, not people.

As we rode in the backseat of the hearse, Joey, Bree, Joe, and I felt a peace that knit our hearts together with heaven. Grace. I can't begin to describe the paradox of joy and sorrow we felt in those moments together.

Back at the church, hundreds of people encircled us with more love, kind words, and hugs as they shared memories and heartfelt tears. People from our church, family, and friends, as well as other people we didn't even know, came together to offer their time, food, service, comfort, and love to us. Heaven came to earth. God gave us a glimpse of the reunions we will have in heaven someday.

Joe compared the spiritual preparation of the funeral to a Billy Graham crusade. Much prayer was offered up by people all over the nation who had heard our story. Is it any wonder His blessings were poured out that day? Psalm 133 says that when God's people dwell in unity, He commands a blessing, even life forever.

It was more than just the girls' funeral. It was their wedding. They joined the Lover of their souls, their heavenly Bridegroom for eternity. God invites mankind to partner with Him as His bride for all eternity, and we get to live it out in this life as His body.

Dear Family and Friends,

We are grateful and overwhelmed by the outpouring of love and generosity by all of you. Through your support and prayers God's grace is being made strong in our weakness. We have such sorrow in our loss, but also great hope that our girls are present with their Lord and Bridegroom, Jesus. We know one day we shall be with them in heaven.

The Lord God bless you,
Joe & Debbie Mayer

A
SERVICE
of

CELEBRATION

OF ETERNAL LIFE

In Loving Memory
Of
Krista, Nikki and Jessica

January 7th, 2004

Funeral program

Joey, Bree, and Debbie singing *I Hear Angels* at funeral

TV news:Three sisters (caskets), three family members singing, three pastors

Joe opening the service with prayer

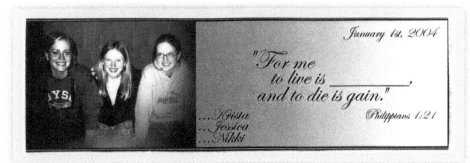

Bookmarks made for the funeral

Caskets at the cemetery

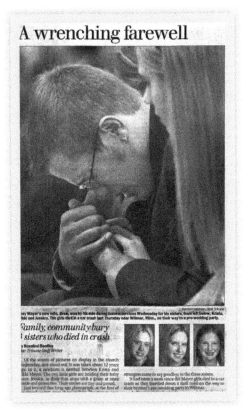

A wrenching farewell

Newspaper the day after the funeral

oy Mayer's new wife, Bree, was by his side during funeral services Wednesday for his sisters, from left below, Krista, iki and Jessica. The girls died in a car crash last Thursday near Willmar, Minn., on their way to a pre-wedding party.

Family, community bury sisters who died in crash

By Rosalind Bentley
Star Tribune Staff Writer

Of the scores of pictures on display in the church Wednesday, one stood out. It was taken about 12 years ago. In it, a newborn is settled between Krista and ikki Mayer. The two little girls are holding their baby sister, Jessica, in their thin arms with a grasp at once gentle and protective. Their smiles are tiny and proud.

Just beyond that long-ago photograph, at the foot of ...

strangers came to say goodbye to the three sisters.

It had been a week since the Mayer girls died in a car crash as they traveled down a dark road on the way to their brother's pre-wedding party in Willmar.

Chapter 12

It Takes a Body

I have never yet known the Spirit of God
to work where the Lord's people were divided.
—Dwight L. Moody

For several years before the accident, we felt a tug to be a part of the larger church body. Together as a family, we prayed for direction for quite some time before leaving the comfort and security of the spiritual family we'd known and loved for over twenty years. The change felt risky but exciting for all of us. Little did we know what being part of the larger body of Christ would be like.

From the minute we heard the devastating news of the accident, people from all over played specific supporting roles, as if each of them had auditioned for a part in the story. In reflection, we saw how God met our needs through His people. This gave us great comfort because we tangibly felt God's love. It brought so much relief to know that the physical needs our tragedy produced were being provided for.

My sister Patty stayed with us for six weeks after the accident. She virtually became my nurse and took care of our home. I had no energy or interest in the details of daily life. But she lived as if my loss was hers. She gave and gave of herself, doing all the things required to run a household. I basically slept (when I could), read our mail, cried, and talked to people. She lived out the words of Jesus about laying down one's life for a friend: "'Greater love has no one than this: to lay down one's life for one's friends'" (John 15:13).

Patty was there when we picked out the girl's headstones, giving reminders of what was important to us. We chose to have roses engraved on them because of the roses Krista had sketched and painted, as well as the many roses we had received. Inscribed on each one was *Beloved Daughter and Sister*, along with the individual Scriptures that represented the girls. She was also with us to see the headstones on the day they arrived, which happened to be the day that would have been Jessica's thirteenth birthday.

People provided for us through acts of kindness such as care baskets, cases of drinking water, flowers, and many nourishing meals (lots of lasagna) that would appear at our doorstep. These gifts came from Christians extending beyond our neighborhood and circle of friends and family. For the first few months, in addition to bringing us meals, people called us, joined us for dinner, and gave us much-needed fellowship and support. Even strangers offered to pray for us and help us in any way we needed.

I spent the first months opening cards with encouraging letters and monetary gifts, recording the names and addresses of those who gave so generously. We received cards, not only from many different states but from other countries as well. Without the outpouring of monetary gifts, we would have faced substantial financial hardship. Because we received so much sympathy and encouragement in daily bundles of mail, close friends and family stepped up to help me by addressing hundreds of thank-you cards.

God continued using the body of Christ at-large to minister to us. One letter came from a woman in South Dakota, saying her prayer group was praying for us and that "we are just one big family." Bundles of handmade cards from school children blessed us. A teacher from one of the many grade schools who reached out to us wrote, "I think [the children] are learning about what it means to be members of the same body."

On a day when I felt particularly down and anxious and was

beginning to wonder if God even heard me or cared, a message came that lit up my darkness in a way only God could orchestrate. Surprisingly, there was only one letter in the mail that day, which seemed to punctuate its value. The writer identified himself as a father of a close-knit family of three daughters and one son who all loved the Lord. He went on to say that we (identifying with our loss) would get through. We would do this by concentrating on two Scriptures that focus on our eyes and God's eyes. He quoted 2 Corinthians 4:18, "So we fix our eyes not on what is seen but on what is unseen. For what is seen is temporary and what is unseen is eternal," and 1 Peter 3:12, "For the eyes of the Lord are on the righteous"—with the added bonus, "His ears are also attentive to our prayers."

This blew me away because of my dark, trying experience from years earlier when God gave me my "Surfing Psalm" (Psalm 18:6, 16, 19): "In my distress I called to the Lord; I cried to my God for help. From his temple he heard my voice; my cry came before him, into his ears. ... He reached down from on high and took hold of me; he drew me out of deep waters. ... He brought me out into a spacious place; he rescued me because he delighted in me."

As these early days wore on, we read letters that contained testimonies of life-changing choices people made and acts done as many souls responded to the Lord, directly as a result of our story. What a privilege to hear about the "working together for good" God brought about after our terrible loss, resulting in spiritual fruit for the kingdom of God that may never have happened otherwise. One of those good things was a prayer group that formed, inspired by the before-school prayer-and-worship time my son and daughters had facilitated at their school.

Numerous stories from family, friends, teachers, and employers expressed how the girls' lives had meaningfully touched their world. A prison inmate, hearing our story, was healed of major losses in his life. A man from Europe, suicidal before hearing the reality of God in our story, surrendered his life and pain to God.

A close friend and neighbor of ours volunteered to create a

memorial website for the girls that provided a meaningful avenue of connection and ministry. The website www.mayersisters.com featured (and still does) portraits of the girls, memorable snapshots of their lives, and such things as their journal pages and artwork. The website was a way for us to minister to others with articles, poems, and songs that told our story, and it became a place where many visitors could come to grieve, as well as receive the hope of eternal life that our story so poignantly offers. Through links to our email and a guestbook, we continued to receive a tremendous number of messages of encouragement and sympathy.

As I think about how the human body works, with each part quickly taking up the slack when another part hurts or is incapacitated or even missing, I see how that is what happened with us. That is what the body of Christ does. It loves.

A local group of Christians formed a prayer group after the funeral. They came together, from eight area churches of different denominations, with the initial reason to pray for the two hundred students who had received Christ at the funeral. The group prayed and cared for my family as well. Together we organized an event, a thank-you night, at one of the local churches so we could publicly thank the area community for their support.

This same group also planned a memorial service/fundraiser concert at St. Anthony High School to remember the girls and raise money for Minnesota Teen Challenge, where I worked prior to the accident. Our desire was to reach out and establish connections for the many young people who attended the funeral. The event featured local bands; Bree and me singing one song; Night Vision, the worship band Joey and Bree were in when they met; and Joel Hanson from the contemporary Christian band PFR.

About thirty young people gave their hearts to the Lord that night. Not only was it an awesome night of sharing music and the gospel message, but the prayer meeting the night before was incredible. Both the fire and police departments helped us with the concert, and many local businesses and a dozen different churches gave their support. Talk about people working together. We glorified Jesus and raised almost $8,000 for Teen Challenge.

The summer after the girls passed, we had a family reunion that my brother planned at a YMCA camp in Missouri. The director of the camp felt moved to dedicate a butterfly garden to my girls, and a beautiful plaque was placed at its entrance. A service was held where Joe shared from Scripture and we planted three dogwood trees in the girls' honor. We have visited the garden several times since, reflecting and honoring the memory of our daughters and the kindness and compassion of so many.

Grief has a way of drawing out love and compassion, enabling us to mourn with those who mourn and weep with those who weep. When one member suffers, we all suffer. We witnessed grief as a catalyst, uniting people to draw comfort from God.

Christians throughout the news media interviewed us and published the story of our girls in numerous magazines and newspapers. Our story was aired on several newscasts that continued for the next three years. God strategically placed Christians in the media to give an account of His story within our smaller one. It was such a paradox to hear about God's love manifested in the midst of such tragedy.

In the first six years, I was invited to many women's events to talk about God's comfort in our lives. Joe spoke with me on occasion at community outreaches. Although we shared mostly throughout Minnesota, we traveled to Missouri, Montana, South and North Dakota, Wisconsin, Iowa, and Hawaii—and abroad to Holland and France. Our brothers and sisters in Christ treated us tenderly everywhere we went. We saw glimpses of how it will be in heaven when we meet people of every tribe and tongue who also love of God. I love the body of Christ!

Whenever possible, Joe or a friend would come along as my hand-holder, for moral and prayer support. By hand-holder, I'm referring to the Old Testament story of a battle in which Moses grew weary holding up the staff of God atop a hill that overlooked the fighting below. Aaron and Hur held up the hands of Moses, giving him the support he needed. As long as they held up his hands, the Israelites rose toward victory. When his hands came down, Israel sank toward defeat. This illustration mirrored my experience when I ministered outside my comfort zone, exemplifying one of the many ways God wants the body of Christ to function. All of these experiences enlarged our understanding of, and appreciation for, the diversity and unity of the body of Christ.

Reflecting on the ways believers came to our side reminded me of a conversation I had with my dad after the last Christmas with our whole family. He commented on how well my kids got along. But just like any other kids, mine did not always get along. It was really the wedding, and the anticipation of it, that created a unique sense of unity between them that Christmas. As a mother, I delighted in his statement, knowing it was God's love producing their unity.

I easily made the jump to wondering how our heavenly Father must have felt while watching His children interact with one another in our story. I believe it hurts Him to see division in the church and delights Him to see unity. I envisioned God declaring to the angels, "Look at my children, My body, My bride. They get along so well. They love each other so much."

Jesus calls believers His family. We are changed by His love, to love one another as we anticipate the great wedding of the Lamb and so produce rare and beautiful treasures to offer a weary and broken world.

Krista's grave marker

Nikki's grave marker

Jessica's grave marker

A visit to the cemetery

Sign for community thank-you service

Sign donated for memorial/benefit concert

Butterfly garden plaque

Moments of grief as Joe shares at
dedication ceremony (sister Kathie and
nephew near Debbie)

Planting trees in honor of the girls' butterfly garden

Part Four

NAVIGATING
THE
WAVE

~ Chapter 13 ~

Eye of the Storm

If peace be in the heart,
the wildest winter storm is full of solemn beauty,
The midnight flash but shows the path of duty,
Each living creature tells some new and joyous story,
The very trees and stones all catch a ray of Glory,
if peace be in the heart.

—CHARLES FRANCIS RICHARDSON

In the days and months following the funeral, I felt alone, so alone without my girls. The anguished cry of my heart went beyond words. My sorrow covered me like a lead blanket. I could barely get out of bed. I wanted to hear giggles, laughter, and the sounds of voices interacting. I ached to hear Jess practicing her clarinet, Nikki rehearsing her voice lessons, or Krista tirelessly sounding out "Für Elise" on our piano. Anything but a silent house punctuated by my endless crying. No familiar sounds of kids getting ready for school or Buddy barking at the commotion of their friends coming through the door. Even he was quiet.

He'd shuffle slowly through the butterfly beads hanging in the doorway of Jessica's bedroom, searching for her but finding only a persistently deserted room. From there he'd go to Nikki's room, sniffing the chair, the bed, and the floor, hoping to find her scent. Then he'd return to me, settle on my lap, and offer his stinky, wet dog

103

kisses as comfort. It worked to some extent, bringing a smile to my face and reminding me of how the kids would joke about his bad dog breath.

I can still remember the joy I felt when each of the kids were born and how much I loved watching their personalities unfold into unique individuals as they grew. I had imagined, prayed, and dreamed about what they would do with their lives, whom they would marry, and how many children they would each have. I pictured family get-togethers with the laughter and fun of a growing family. I envisioned how God would touch the world through them. Like any other parent, my children were an extension of me. But then—so abruptly—they were gone. The future I dreamed of would never be.

I needed to sense God's presence. Without it I would give up.

Perhaps, in a small way, it was my love and concern for Joey and Bree that gave me the incentive to hope for whatever I could find hope in during that first year. Yes, Joey gained two brothers-in-law, but he lost the siblings he grew up with and the family as he had always known. Bree would never have the three sisters she was so excited to gain.

Caring about others generates something redemptive and purposeful. Not wanting our family to become a total casualty of loss prevented me from being sucked into an abyss of despair. This desire gave me incentive to hold on.

As overwhelming as the storm of emotions was in us and everyone around us, we felt undeniably held in God's strong arms. It was so supernatural that people wondered if we were in a state of denial. Some said we were being unrealistic and would soon fall apart. The truth is we had already fallen apart. Our world had crashed around us, and we relied on God to carry us.

In the early stages of grief, God provides an emotional cushion, a kind of shock absorber, if you will. This miraculous design within our souls helps us slowly absorb the truth that our loved ones are gone, giving our emotions time to process what our mind already knows. I never denied the fact that my girls were gone; too much reminded me of their absence, but my feelings were raw and exposed, so God provided this cushion to protect me from being overcome by grief.

In the devotional book *Streams in the Desert*, by L. B. Cowman, I read about the "cushion of the sea." This cushion is in the deep regions where water is still, and vegetation and animals find protection from raging storms that sweep across the ocean. Once, a submarine undergoing a test remained underwater for many hours. After returning to the harbor, the captain was asked how the storm affected them. The sub had been so far beneath the surface that it had reached the cushion of the sea. He said he wasn't even aware there had been a storm.

It was in this undisturbed calm that my spirit remained for quite a while. The circumstances had not changed. My thoughts and emotions still raged. But in the deepest part of me, where God's presence dwells, I felt safe and secure.

When winds of a tropical storm increase to extremely high winds, the air above sinks into the center of the storm, causing a calm—this is called "the eye of the storm." The weather inside the eye is calm and sunny. A person can even sunbathe in the eye of a storm, but surrounding the eye is its spinning wall, where the most violent winds of the storm blows. Our storm, with its violent winds of emotion, raged all around us, but our hearts stayed calm, still with God's peace. We were secure in the eye of our storm.

In the days that followed the accident, we received a card from some good friends. The image on the cover of the card pictured Peter sinking in storm-tossed waves as the wind and rain intimidated him. Jesus, with an outstretched hand, was pulling him up from the threatening waves. That card stayed on my refrigerator for more than four years, reminding me that Jesus is with me in my stormy waters to lift me up each time I start to sink. Over the last few years, I've learned a lot about my storm through Matthew 14:22–33:

> Immediately He made the disciples get into the boat and go ahead
> of Him to the other side, while He sent the crowds away. After
> He had sent the crowds away, He went up on the mountain by

Himself to pray; and when it was evening, He was there alone. But the boat was already a long distance from the land, battered by the waves; for the wind was contrary. And in the fourth watch of the night He came to them, walking on the sea. When the disciples saw Him walking on the sea, they were terrified, and said, "It is a ghost!" And they cried out in fear. But immediately Jesus spoke to them, saying, "Take courage, it is I; do not be afraid." Peter said to Him, "Lord, if it is You, command me to come to You on the water." And He said, "Come!" And Peter got out of the boat, and walked on the water and came toward Jesus. But seeing the wind, he became frightened, and beginning to sink, he cried out, "Lord, save me!" Immediately Jesus stretched out his hand and took hold of him, and said to him, "You of little faith, why did you doubt?" When they got into the boat, the wind stopped. And those who were in the boat worshiped Him, saying, "You are certainly God's Son!" (NASB)

Jesus had told the disciples to get into the boat and go to the other side of the lake ahead of Him. The disciples did just what He told them to do, but the storm still came. At times I was tempted to think I must not have been in God's will for such a tragedy to strike. It was easier to believe I had done something wrong to deserve what happened than to think a good God would allow it to happen. Satan, the accuser of the brethren, was right there, screaming accusations in my ear, telling me it was my fault—that I was a bad mother, that I must have been for this to have happened.

Because we are human, we have a limited understanding of things that happen in this life, and we can beat ourselves up trying to make sense of what we don't understand. Some things will only be clear when we see Jesus face-to-face. Looking back on my life, I realized it's not as if I'm trusting someone I know nothing about. This is the God who loves me. If He loved me so much that He gave His only Son to die for me, I can certainly trust Him with His eternal purposes.

Verse 25 says that Jesus didn't come to the disciples until the fourth watch, which is early morning when it is still dark. It was definitely my darkest moment when I heard the news of the accident. I was completely overwhelmed by the darkness of my circumstances.

When it's the darkest, I have found, I have greater opportunity to exercise my faith because it requires me to believe without seeing. Yet it is just as easy for God to move in my life when it is dark as when it is light. Psalm 139:12 tells me that "even the darkness will not be dark to you; the night will shine like the day, for darkness is as light to you."

In my darkest, most desperate moment, I sensed God more than ever. He came, giving me images and memories of the past, while offering me glimpses of the future reminding me of eternity with tokens from heaven.

My greatest faith is expressed and strengthened while trusting that He sees and knows exactly when and what I need—especially when it is dark and I cannot see.

Naturally, I didn't walk through this with flying colors, but I felt comforted that the disciples didn't either. In the scene of Jesus walking on the stormy sea, His disciples had just witnessed the miracle of Jesus feeding the five thousand. Still, they didn't recognize Him—it was dark and scary; all they could do was cry out in fear at the ghost they thought they saw coming toward them.

Everything about this grief journey was foreign to both Joe and me. How could God be in this? Too much tragedy. Too much heartbreak. Too much fright.

I was used to experiencing God in safer, more comfortable circumstances, like worshiping at church, having devotions, being with friends, or enjoying family times. But when we gathered to pray in our living room the night of the accident, God came to me, even as I repeated over and over, "What am I going to do?" I didn't recognize Him at first because I was terrified. It was too dark. Too horrible.

He said the very same thing to me as He did to the disciples when He showed me the picture of my girls as His brides and the Scripture in Krista's journal from Philippians 1:21: "For me to live is Christ, to die is gain." He spoke it again when I read in Nikki's Bible about our hearts being where our treasure is found. He said, "Take courage, it is I!"

Later, a few weeks after the funeral, when I was still utterly overwhelmed with grief and sorrow, I was looking for something under my bed when I came across the painting Joey gave me on New Year's Day—a bride and groom, representing Jesus and His bride, the church. Stunned by the fact that He had given me that specific painting the very day my girls became the Lord's brides in heaven, I sensed the Lord saying once again, "Take courage, it is I!"

The disciples were terrified of the stormy water and waves. They believed they would surely drown. Everything was out of their control, but Jesus showed them He was in control. He demonstrated His authority over the storm by walking to them on the very water they expected would drown them. He was greater than what they feared.

Like the disciples, Jesus came to me in the worst storm of my life to show me He is always in control over any fearful expectations I have. Our girls died, and yet He is even in control of death. Because He has risen, I know He has power over the grave. Although my girls died, I know from John 11:25 that they live.

At times I thought I would surely drown in sorrow, afraid I couldn't go on with my life. A month after the accident, nearing Jessica's thirteenth birthday, I was lying in bed, paralyzed with fear and tears. I anxiously wondered how I would be able to make it through the many more birthdays and holidays still to come, let alone get out of bed that day.

On the nightstand beside me I noticed a gospel tract on top of my Bible. It must have come in one of the many sympathy cards we received. I reached for it and was met with the wisdom to take each day at a time, breaking it down to hours, then minutes, reassuring me that God was there to help me through each one, down to the very second. It was exactly what I needed to get out of bed that day. Jesus comforted me with His overwhelming presence and peace, reminding me He is in control of my past, present, and future—and through His words of hope, I learned He is stronger than any of my fears.

In Matthew 14:28, Peter walked on water to Jesus. But before getting out of the boat, he said, "If it is you, tell me to come to you on the water." Jesus told him to come, yet Peter had no ability of his own to walk on water. At times it seemed that God was asking me to do things beyond my own ability, like walking on water.

The night of the rehearsal dinner, after seeing my girls' bodies on the tables in the hospital, my heart was crushed, but God gave me supernatural strength to stand before the news cameras and microphones and declare my faith and trust in God. Without any forethought, He literally put words into Joe's and my mouths that brought the world's attention to life beyond this one. It's truly amazing what we are able to do when our gaze is on Him. He called me to Himself and enabled me to do what was beyond me.

The storm continued, and as Peter began to focus on the wind and waves, he took his eyes off Jesus and began to sink, calling out to Him, "Lord, save me!" Jesus immediately stretched out His hand. "You of little faith, why did you doubt?" He wasn't condemning Peter for sinking. He was reminding Peter that He had personally spoken to him and that he shouldn't have doubted.

The Lord wasn't asking Peter to do anything in his own strength, nor was He asking me to do anything in mine. He wanted me to recall what He had so intimately told me.

Jesus had whispered beautiful words into my heart about eternal life and eternal treasures the night the girls became His brides. I realized if I were to focus on my loss instead of His words, I would be overcome with fear and sink in waves of despair. Many times I cried out to Him, "Lord, save me!" And He would mercifully take my hand, remind me of His words, and pull me out of the raging water.

I think Jesus is more concerned about our relationship with Him than He is about our walking on water. He wants us aware of His presence and to listen to His voice. He knows that the minute our focus strays from Him and His words to our circumstances, we begin to sink into waves of doubt and unbelief.

Storms gradually die down, but when Jesus got into the boat, the winds instantly ceased and the waves calmed. Jesus not only demonstrated His power by walking on water, He did it while the winds still blew and the waves still tossed. He loves to take our breath away with His power and presence in the midst of our storms. The disciples were so amazed that they worshiped Him, declaring Him "God's Son."

Just ten days after my girls passed, our good friends Mike and Char came to visit. Char and I had led worship together for years. Char sat at the piano and began to play, and I picked up my guitar to play along. Mike and Patty joined us in singing praises to Jesus. We were so completely aware of God's presence and peace that our hearts were filled with joy. As we worshiped, we truly felt as if we touched heaven, acknowledging and so declaring Jesus was God's Son.

Although Jesus was not physically present to comfort us, as He was with the disciples, we knew He was with us. Just before His crucifixion, He promised His disciples that God's "Helper" would come, calling Him the "Spirit of truth."

Jesus promised to be with us until the end of age and that He would not leave us as orphans. Although my girls were gone, I knew I was not alone. I had the Holy Spirit as my helper and guide. Even in the midst of my storm, I experienced supernatural peace. Romans 5:1 tells me I am justified by faith and have peace with God through our Lord Jesus Christ. When I am aware of His presence, and in right relationship with Him, I can have peace no matter what the circumstances are. My inner peace comes from being at peace with God, not by finding peaceful circumstances. That is what carried me through the months following the loss of our girls. I was unmistakably safe in the eye of the storm.

Card that hung on the fridge for over four years

[*Refuge and Strength,* copyright Morgan Weistling www.morganweistling.com]

Chapter 14

In the Aftermath

Grief is like the ocean, it comes in waves, ebbing and flowing.
Sometimes the water is calm, and sometimes it is overwhelming.
All we can do is learn to swim.

—Vicki Harrison

When a natural disaster hits, it can leave behind a trail of devastation. Our loss was an emotional tsunami that radically changed the landscape of our lives, leaving wreckage and wiping out familiar landmarks. When we are not aware of the potential danger after a personal inundation, the successive waves can build with the potential to bring total devastation. Thankfully, we became aware of possible aftereffects.

We needed to be alert.

My brother-in-law and several others warned us of potential danger and urged us to get counseling for our marriage. We were told the statistics of breakups after tragedies are high.

After a tidal wave hits, people are advised to head for higher ground to avoid succeeding waves. After our wave, we made a beeline for higher ground, which was Jesus, our firm foundation. We prayed and asked God to strengthen us, both as individuals and as a couple. Following our brother-in-law's advice, Joe scheduled counseling for himself after the first month. He wanted professional and objective input to help him process his thoughts and emotions. I quickly followed for several sessions together.

In our broken states, we often expressed our pain in ways that sometimes brought hurt and division to our relationship. As a result, we needed to give each other grace to grieve in our unique ways. We had learned early in our marriage that if we were not honest with each other, resentment could grow. But we remembered the truth that our struggle was not with each other, but with Satan: "For our struggle is not against flesh and blood, but against the rulers, against the authorities, against the powers of this dark world and against the spiritual forces of evil in the heavenly realms" (Ephesians 6:12). We endeavored to communicate our feelings in a kind manner to prevent allowing any opportunity the enemy might use to capitalize on the vulnerability of our devastating circumstances.

The Father, Son, and Holy Spirit have always existed in perfect unity and harmony, having no competition in their divine rolls. As children of God created in His image, we too were made to reflect that unity in our relationships with one another, especially in the context of Christian marriage. According to Ephesians 5, the relationship between a husband and wife is comparable to the relationship between Christ and His bride—the church. That unity needs to be intentionally protected. Joe and I took extra care not to take each other, or God, for granted, reminding ourselves that our battles were not only with our human weaknesses, but with spiritual forces of darkness contending against our love and unity.

I learned early on in my walk with God that when I place my hope in anything but Him, I set myself up for disappointment. Only as Joe and I individually depended on God to heal us were we able to encourage and support each other. None of us were created to be made whole by another person, nor by favorable circumstances.

One of the Scripture verses read at our wedding was, "Though one may be overpowered, two can defend themselves. A cord of three strands is not quickly broken" (Ecclesiastes 4:12). In a healthy marriage, if life is going well, one spouse is usually able to encourage the other when he or she is down. However, when an emotional storm hits them at once, both are weak and hurting. That's when we need the third person—Jesus.

For years, I had depended on Joe to be the steady one. But now he was as broken, weak, and vulnerable as I was. Both of us hurt and were unable to ignore our pain, which changed the dynamics of our relationship. Because of the glaring differences of how we expressed ourselves, we could easily misunderstand each other. But as we were open and honest with each other, we could pour out our hearts to God together. In doing this, God touched us in ways that only He could, enabling us to realize we were truly *for* each other. There were days we did well, and there were days we didn't do well at all. But we always had the next day to begin again.

Because of God's help, our marriage became stronger than it was before our storm. If having a home safety plan can determine your destruction or survival during and after a damaging storm, I can attest the same about our spiritual home safety plan. I am so thankful for our firm foundation in Jesus that prevented our destruction. The storm that took half of my family, and a major part of all that was familiar, did shake us. But because of the grace of God, it did not wipe us out!

Horatio Spafford wrote the familiar hymn "It is Well with My Soul" after the deaths of his four daughters at sea. He described grief's aftermath accurately in the line, "When sorrows like sea billows roll." Emotional aftershocks have no compassion or sympathy. They are cruel and merciless, coming at unguarded and gullible moments. These waves and aftereffects acted as triggers that seemed to sweep over me with no warning in the first few years, but in time, I learned to prepare myself for them.

At first, whenever an event such as a celebration, out-of-town company, or a speaking engagement would come to an end, sorrow came crashing down on me like a tidal wave. I felt a sense of loss as if I were experiencing it all for the first time. Just like the billowing waves of the sea, I couldn't stop them or subdue them.

Each time Joe left the house, a wave of panic would tempt me with fear that he would not return. *After all,* I would think, *if God allowed my girls to die, and I could make it, why not Joe too? Maybe God thinks I can handle that as well.*

For some time, whenever I drove my car, especially at night, it triggered an instant replay of how I envisioned the accident had been. I saw myself in the car with them, in the unsuspecting horror of their last moments on earth. Saw the oncoming headlights. Felt the impact. Sometimes I had to pull over and stop driving.

Also, whenever I saw an accident on the road involving an ambulance, I'd be so shaken I'd have to pull over because tears would blur my vision. In time, though, I learned to take those kinds of thoughts captive to the truths God had spoken about my girls' eternal life, choosing to allow His peace to fill my heart and mind. I endeavored to rely on the underlying truth that God deeply loves me. I eventually began to pray for the people involved in the accidents I would drive by.

I'd hear a song, or someone would speak or act like one of the girls, triggering an overwhelming sorrow all over again. While taking a walk in the park by our house one day, a couple of girls walked on the other side of a stream that flowed between us. One of them giggled and moved much like Jessica would have. My heart skipped a beat, and I wanted to run after them. Instead, with tears flowing, whispering Jessica's name, I cried out to God until the wave of sorrow subsided.

While in a fitting room, I heard a mother and daughter in the next compartment laughing and debating which clothes to buy. It immobilized me. Tears were my only expression until I could regain my composure. This happened many times.

I would put off grocery shopping, because whenever I went, I was reminded of all the things I didn't need to buy anymore. If my sudden attack of grief didn't happen in the cereal or snack aisle, I'd burst into tears at the checkout. Right when I thought I was stronger and felt prepared for the task, something else would blindside me. It took time—as in years—but eventually I could get from dairy to vegetables to the parking lot without falling apart.

The first few times I had to buy a greeting card was no different. I don't know how I didn't anticipate the mother/daughter section, but it caught me off guard and I would have to rush out to my car to avoid drawing attention to my emotional breakdowns.

There was one very special time when the card isle comforted me though. I had developed a tradition of listening to The Chronicles of Narnia books on CD during every Christmas season. Jess had fallen in love with these books at age ten when her teacher read them aloud in class. We also listened on Saturday mornings to Focus on the Family's presentation of the audio version. She absolutely loved Narnia, so this became a special way to celebrate Jess. Listening to these CDs took me to another place and reminded me that my real home is not here, connecting me with the girls as I listened.

The third New Year's came with major disappointments and struggles. I would imagine being comforted by Aslan (representing Jesus), as if climbing up on his mane. He'd defend me with a roar and take me for a ride on his back as he did for Susan and Lucy in the story. After a particularly discouraging day, a friend listened compassionately as I told her about my struggles. She prayed for me, unaware of my present obsession with Narnia. "Jesus, please show yourself to Debbie as the Lion of Judah and roar for her in her defense against the demons of hell coming against her." I could almost hear Aslan roar.

I went to the bookstore the next day to buy a card for someone, and as I walked past the clearance rack, I saw a picture of a lion roaring. No kidding. Sure enough, it was Aslan. I opened the card and it said, *No winter lasts forever. Be encouraged, there are better days ahead for you!* This time, I cried tears of joy. I bought the card and placed it on my dresser, and there it sat for about a year. My card from Jesus.

At times I would have to leave a church service. On one occasion, being fairly new to our church, I didn't see any of the people I knew. A guest speaker talked about the blessings of his four children and fourteen grandchildren. Being surrounded by families, he went on describing his "blessed family." I became cruelly aware that I would never have a lot of grandchildren. It was so in my face that Joe and I were not sitting next to our girls—or anyone else we felt close to. I slid headlong into a vortex of loneliness and could hardly breathe until I stumbled out of the row toward the door.

Of course, it didn't help that the previous day I was looking at our last family Christmas photo, remembering how I had imagined many future family photos, especially after Joey's wedding, thinking our numbers would be doubled with spouses and then multiplied with grandchildren. As I thought about our upcoming Christmas photo, my heart sank, knowing it would only have four heartbroken individuals in the picture.

In moments such as these, it was hard to think of us as a family. I felt misplaced and alone—painfully aware of my broken family—and feeling as though no one really knew me.

Joe expressed that even if the whole world were hugging us, it would never be the same as having our girls to hug and being a whole family again. This actually presented us with a beautiful picture of how our heavenly Father feels toward each of us. No one can substitute the unique place and relationship God desires for each one He's created. Grasping that truth made me feel better and gave me a better perspective.

More aftermath came in the form of altered relationships. Our friendships were not destroyed, but many were clouded with uncertainty. There were several different ways in which this dynamic played out.

At first, I felt more like a celebrity than a mourner, exceptionally loved and even sought-after. I knew people genuinely loved and cared for me, but oftentimes, when I went to a place where people had known my girls, I would be bombarded with greetings and hugs. I believe that to see me was, in a sense, a representation of the girls in a huggable, physical way. At other times, and for the very same reason, I felt people avoided me. I think I was too much of a reminder of the frailty and uncertainty of life.

I believe what happened in my life challenged the convictions of some in what they believed about God: *Why would a good God allow something like this to happen? If this happened to the Mayers, it could also happen to me.* Seeing me made people confront questions that required them to rethink their theology.

We tend to want answers for everything that happens, and when we don't get them, we're uncomfortable. We want life—and death—to make sense. When there seems to be no apparent answers, we realize that we are not the ones in control. And we do not like that.

Our culture is uncomfortable with grief and prolonged pain. Because of that, people can say things that, instead of bringing comfort, heap on more pain. I'm sure I've done the same to others. When asked how I was feeling, I would respond honestly and say, "Very sad," or "I miss my girls so much." Meaning well, people would respond, "Oh, but your girls are in a much better place," or "You'll see them again one day," or "Well, at least you don't have to pray for them anymore." All true, but not comforting. Not at all.

The more immediate truth was I just needed my feelings validated. That's all anyone really needs after a loss. Grief is about a broken heart. It is a normal response to loss. Jesus never condemns us for our feelings. He accepts us where we're at and sympathizes with our pain—then He speaks truth. But it's always in that order. That's why He came to live as a man—to identify with us.

It wasn't so much what people would say, but how they said it. Before hurting people can be open to advice, they need to know that someone is truly listening to their hearts. Some interactions with people were just plain awkward. It was hard to talk about lighthearted things like the weather. I saw nothing lighthearted about my life. I think people were afraid of making me cry. But the truth is, that's about all I was capable of doing for a while. A long while. I confess, I was pretty intense to be around.

This was a new experience. Not just for me, but my friends as well. I believed a lot of my friends and family wanted to interact with me as they always had in the past, sharing the enjoyment of life rather than the sorrow of loss. This (sometimes false) perception of not having what people wanted from me would hit me, and I would construct an invisible wall before a word was spoken. Other times, it was obvious that people were avoiding an encounter with me.

I began to think about how I might respond if I were in other people's shoes. Then I recognized my responsibility. Part of the package of grief is to create a bridge for people. As difficult as it was at first, God gave me grace to reach out in uncomfortable situations, to build bridges so people didn't feel so awkward with me.

Reaching beyond myself to others became part of my healing. That does not mean all my interactions and attempts to reach out were successful. Many times the waves of grief overtook me, and I simply walked away feeling helpless, hurt, or misunderstood. Other times, I avoided situations entirely. I gradually learned to navigate the strange waters of grief. But it's a journey, and every journey takes time.

Whether I liked it or not, normal events continued on, which meant graduations, weddings, and school performances. The first wedding I went to was the summer after the girls' deaths. One of Krista's best friends was getting married, and Krista would have been in the wedding party. I was genuinely happy for the couple, but not seeing Krista as a bridesmaid triggered not just tears but a deluge of them—right there in the church sanctuary. The same thing happened at Nikki's end-of-year choir concert and then at Jessica's band concert.

The events continued: graduations, showers, more weddings, and then baby showers. Each one came with its own teeter-totter of anticipation and dread, happiness, and sadness. I truly wanted to be a part of my friends' celebrations. Each time I thought I could handle it,

I'd be hit unexpectedly by my emotions. Once the first tear fell, the floodgates opened. I hated that. I wondered if I would ever be able to go to a wedding or baby shower without having to leave the room to cry or leave altogether. Would I ever be able to fully rejoice with anyone again?

Even when surrounded by people, I felt lonely. Nothing anyone said or did was ever good enough, because nothing could bring my girls back. Being with old friends only accentuated the girls' absence. I felt as if people only wanted to be with my girls—and so did I! On the other hand, my new friendships seemed empty, because they didn't know my girls, which magnified my loss even more.

Some friendships were put on hold, and some ended, which felt like abandonment to me. Thankfully, I had some friends who always showed love and support and were not afraid of my tragic loss or pain.

Family events were no different. As our initial shock wore off, extended family interactions felt dysfunctional. The absence of Krista's amusing antics, Jessica's silly laughter, and Nikki's calm responses seemed to shout louder than the endless chatter that seemed like an attempt to make up for their absence. When I finally realized my extended family members were just grieving in a different way than I was, I could lower my expectations of them.

When it came to Joe, me, Joey, and Bree, I sensed major gaps in our relating and conversing. All the roles, dynamics, and communication patterns of our relationships seemed to be off-kilter. I don't think any of us had a clue how to get them back. We each expressed our pain so uniquely. This wave knocked me over several times, and I had to be mindful not to let it pull me under.

I eventually learned that if I expected everyone to grieve as I did, it actually built walls between us. It took time for me to understand that our differences were not personal attacks on me and that their experiences were as legitimate as mine. I had to let them grieve in their own way. With time, communication, honesty, humility, openness, and vulnerability, we began to regain our equilibrium as a family. Today, I feel our family is stronger because of it.

In the beginning, many people came to Jesus and experienced God in new ways, all due to our story. Each testimony of a changed life encouraged us that something good came out of our tragedy. Sadly, we heard that later on some of those same people became embittered and turned to drugs or other destructive behaviors. This news cruelly translated to more grief in my heart. My own thoughts, like a lying messenger, reasoned that the girls died for nothing.

After some time, I found comfort in the promise of Isaiah 55:11: "So is my word that goes out from my mouth: It will not return to me empty, but will accomplish what I desire and achieve the purpose for which I sent it." God's Word, like the rain that waters the earth and brings forth seed, will not return void.

I thought back to when I first received the truth of God's Word. First it had to be planted in my heart. It wasn't instant life. I needed to see my need. The seed took time and eventually blossomed. To this day, I pray for those who are still in a place of pain and uncertainty about the deaths of my girls. I know that God will never give up on those who responded to Him at that time.

Grief's waves can sweep in unexpectedly and fiercely, as described in the song lyric "when sorrows like sea billows roll." Even today, waves of grief come and go—sometimes they are harsh, knocking me off my feet; other times they are gentle, like I'm being washed.

I learned early on that I needed to take the necessary steps to rebuild while navigating through my journey of grief and that the grieving process would be lifelong but at the same time filled with God's love and presence.

Chapter 15

One Step at a Time

*Sometimes the smallest step in the right direction
ends up being the biggest step of your life.
Tiptoe if you must, but take the step.*

—NAEEM CALLAWAY

I knew rebuilding my life would involve sifting through the rubble of broken thoughts and emotions. I wanted to do what I could to discover and reshape my so-called "new normal."

Grief is a journey that continues to happen in increments of time, bringing us to new levels of wholeness. It is never just an event. The process overlaps and involves many steps—some smaller, some bigger.

At first, I could barely think clearly enough to read Scripture. I mostly just cried. My tears pleaded, "Help me! Hold me!"

I read the same Scriptures over and over, seeking constant assurance of God's love. In one way, I was like an infant who needed to be sustained and nurtured to survive. In another way, I was like a critically ill patient who needed personal care and life support to go on. But gradually, a baby learns to be independent and a recovering patient learns to breathe without a respirator. The grief process is gradual as well, and it happens one step at a time.

In the early days of my grief, I hardly gave thought to what I did each day because my sister cared for me for six weeks. After she returned to her own life, I took baby steps, which required great effort, to take care of myself enough to get through each day.

God desires to bring healing to the whole person—body, mind, and spirit. He created each part as a whole. I tried to eat properly, get enough rest, and drink plenty of water, which wasn't too hard because a dear friend gave me cases of bottled water. Some days I didn't do a thing except what was needed to survive.

Those were the days I made a list, thankful for the advice I'd been given. The list served as a reminder and motivator that life still went on. I did as author and speaker Elisabeth Elliot advised: "When you don't know what to do next, just do the thing in front of you."[4] *I had to make lists because things* like making phone calls, vacuuming, laundry, and errands overwhelmed me. If I could scratch just one or two of these off my list each day, I felt accomplished.

Of course, the thing in front of you can be the hardest thing—like getting out of bed. The next thing would be to make my bed and get dressed, maybe. Then make a cup of coffee and eventually breakfast. A warm bath and a good book became a nightly ritual for four years. I learned the importance of being kind and occasionally pampering myself, especially when life stunk so bad.

These simple tasks of tending to my physical needs reminded my mind and emotions that I was still alive while reassuring me that I was not going crazy. Buddy's tail-wagging presence was always therapeutic at those times. One of the baby steps on my to-do list was to make sure I fed him and took him on little walks; he needed attention too.

Some days the thing in front of me was simply to listen to praise music—to soak in God's presence instead of self-pity. Once, on a bleak winter's day, I was lying on my living room couch, aware that my tears might drown me. I put on a CD of instrumental piano worship, and as it played, the peaceful notes filled the room, soothing and consoling my spirit like sweet medicine. I gazed through the ice crystals that had formed on our big picture window and saw that it was snowing again. In that moment, the grief in my heart felt as relentless and unchanging as the winter outside.

But then I noticed the snowflakes glistening in the sun. They seemed to be dancing, cheerfully falling to the earth, becoming a fresh, beautiful blanket of snow on the ground. They showed me that things can and will change. As I watched the snow, the Holy Spirit whispered into my spirit the words of Lamentations 3:22: "Because of the Lord's great love we are not consumed, for his compassions never fail."

The snowflakes, new and fresh, were like God's tender mercies that fall on the ground of my heart. He reminded me that because of His great love, I would not be consumed. That small step of putting on praise music not only gave me fresh perspective but also birthed a song I would later write about God's faithfulness.

Being patient with myself was sometimes the biggest step of all. Well-meaning people were prone to offer suggestions about my grieving process, but I could only do what I was ready to do—and being ready is different for each person who has lost someone.

Krista had been living on her own with a girlfriend, so we had to move her belongings from her place to ours early on. There it all sat in the middle of our family room. We had no choice but to go through her things and decide what to keep and what to give away.

The little steps gradually became bigger and involved more of my emotions, until I could face going through one of the girls' closets or dressers, deciding what to do with their clothes and personal belongings. The thought overwhelmed me. So I had to break it down to one girl, one task at a time, one day at a time. Joe helped me.

The year after the girls' deaths, hundreds of refugees from Hurricane Katrina came to Minnesota to regroup. I had not been able to let go of the girls' winter coats and some of their clothes until I learned of the needs of so many refugees. Both Joe and I knew the girls would be happy to share their things, so giving away their coats became a positive experience for us.

Over a four-year period, I tackled more things left in Jess's and Nikki's rooms—little by little. Joey and Bree and other close family and friends chose and kept items that meant something to them.

After the first year, I hosted a slumber party with some of Jessica's friends to sort through her clothes and personal items. Each of them took a few special items. We made it into a fun time and watched a movie, because that was something Jess would have done with them.

Nikki's friends came over one at a time, and while we went through her things together, they'd share their special interactions and memories about Nikki as they related to the items they chose. It meant a lot to Joe and me that the girls' friends wanted keepsakes as special memories of them—but this, too, had to come in increments of time.

Nikki was frugal with her money and, for a seventeen-year-old, had a substantial amount in her savings account. We chose to bless a special-needs group home where she had worked. We donated her money there so that a couple of the residents could attend a Christian summer camp. These were positive steps on our journey toward healing.

A lot of the things I had once enjoyed seemed meaningless. I longed for the pain to end, convinced it never would. I often argued with myself to not just curl up on the couch because I knew I'd feel worse if I gave into that temptation. Both Joe and I learned that as we took steps to do things that brought us enjoyment, we stayed connected to the girls. We knew they'd want us to have fun and be physically active; they would not want us to be inactive and sad.

We had always enjoyed playing tennis as a family, so we made it a priority to keep up with it, and Joey and Bree often joined us. Working in my garden, taking walks by the lake, and hiking were activities that helped me re-embrace life.

One weekend Joe and I took a trip to Wabasha, Minnesota. While walking along an embankment by Lake Pepin, we thought of Jessica. Her favorite thing to do on a hike was to take a detour from the trail to explore. While stooping down to pick up a rock, I felt a prodding, almost as real as a nudge on my shoulder, to turn around. As I did, I saw the most beautiful sunset. We wondered if the girls were in on the experience. The mysterious occasion prompted a series of questions I often asked the girls in my heart. Here is the song those questions produced, called "What Is It Like?"

What is it like to see the face of God?

How does it feel to walk the streets of gold?

What is it like bowing down before the Throne?

How does it feel to have heaven as your home?

How does it feel? What is it like? What do you do?

What is it like to dance before the King?

How does it feel when He begins to sing?

What is it like when all of heaven joins along?

How does it feel to sing love's eternal song?

How does it feel? What is it like? What do you do?

I know—we can only imagine having heaven as our home.

But when I spend some time with Jesus,

I can know Him and be known,

And I feel so right at home.

As I glimpse eternity, with my King I want to be.

What do you do each time He looks at you?

What do you say each time He speaks to you?

How does it feel each time He touches you?

What is it like to behold the King of love?

How does it feel? What is it like? What do you do?

Within the first month, we took the step of seeing a counselor. That brought objective accountability and affirmation to both of us, which helped us know we were on the right track spiritually and emotionally, and that we should keep it up. We also attended the prayer and support group in our community that had formed to pray for the kids who had made decisions to follow Christ at the funeral. This helped us stay connected where God could give us needed love and support. The care from other believers in our community was like an anchor for our souls.

The following spring, we joined a grief group that met at our church. This also was a helpful step that connected us with others who had experienced loss. A couple of very entertaining people in the group kept us all laughing. A passerby would never have guessed we were a grief group by the sounds of us. Laughter and comic relief does wonders to heal, as Proverbs 17:22 proved true: "A cheerful heart is good medicine, but a crushed spirit dries up the bones."

These support groups were steps in our journey, lifelines in the process of grieving. I learned rather quickly to surround myself with people who could listen at an intimate level without feeling uncomfortable or intimidated by my pain. I determined to be with individuals who loved and nurtured me until my initial pain subsided and I grew strong enough to reach out to others beyond my safe circle. How long that took, I don't remember. In grief, everything overlaps while morphing into a new normal.

I discovered it's not what we do, but what happens inside of us and how we respond to our loss that is what really matters. Staying connected to others provided a safety net, especially from isolating and withdrawing, which I constantly wanted to do.

Joe and I continued serving and staying connected with others at our church. This naturally involved reaching out to people. There's always someone else who is hurting. God placed a capacity within each of us to care about someone else, even if it is just a friendly smile. An important step in the grief process is to get our eyes off our own pain. We were created to walk in love—not just talk about it.

Another major step I took was a trip back to Willmar. I had initially promised myself I would never drive on the same road where the girls had died, hoping to never see the town again. That lasted a few years, until a friend of the girls ended up in a drug treatment facility in

Willmar and asked us to visit him. I thought for sure I would fall apart when we came to the spot of the accident, and I braced myself for it.

Surprisingly, it turned into a wonderful moment. As my stomach churned and tears erupted, my heart told me that this was the spot where my girls met Jesus face-to-face. At once, my entire perspective changed. What I thought would be eerie and grievous became beautiful and healing. Had I refused to face the scene of the accident, I may never have shared that sweet, insightful moment with Jesus.

I never initiated any of my speaking engagements, but they became a big step and very healing as I shared our story and the details of God's consistent faithfulness. Talking about my girls and what God was doing energized me.

Not everyone has the desire or the opportunity to share their story publicly, but having some avenue to communicate one's experience is an important step. Although everyone expresses grief differently, all who grieve need a way to express it. Encouraging someone to "give words to your grief" is like encouraging a crying, frustrated child to "use your words." It can help. Our words allow us to identify our feelings and gain perspective. They also encourage and teach others as we invite them into our experience.

. For years I had wanted to record a CD of songs I had written. Never did I imagine that the platform would be the girls' going to heaven. Within the first couple of years after the accident, I wrote and performed several songs birthed from God's personal comfort. When I started receiving requests for a CD, I eventually saw the value of producing one, and a friend from church offered free studio time to me to start the project. I began recording *Eternity Calls,* a CD to honor my girls and God. As it turned out, God connected me with others to produce it.

Although the music CD was not accomplished without struggle, recording it proved one of the more significant steps I took in my healing journey. It required perseverance, hard work, patience, and a lot of prayer. For the CD, Joey wrote a stirring, passionate song for Jessica, and Bree brought her beautiful voice to the mix. Another song came from a friend who imagined what it might have been like when the girls met Jesus. Since I had saved recordings of all three girls singing, I added these clips to several songs. We also created a DVD with two music videos and a short documentary of our story.

Ironically, on the night the girls died, I'd thought I'd never be able to sing again. As it was, the making of the CD became a testimony to God's faithfulness and taught me to never say never. All these activities, tasks, and efforts meant life continued and hadn't ended for me after all. These steps I took helped me begin to regain life and the new normal I knew God intended for me to live.

Chapter 16

Snapshots, Videos, Cassette Tapes, and Memories

What we have once enjoyed we can never lose.
All that we deeply love becomes a part of us.
—HELEN KELLER

Grief is internal. It is the emotional reaction to the loss of someone we loved and the special relationship we had with them. Mourning is the outward expression of that grief. We all grieve when someone we love dies, but mourning is a choice we make if we want to heal.

I had the crying part down pretty well. But I needed to find another way to mourn. My puffy eyes, exhaustion, and lingering headaches pleaded with me to try something else. Talking came naturally, but that too became exhausting.

I'm a creative person who thrives on projects, and so I found unique ways to mourn. I still cried, but when I began journaling, scrapbooking, and talking to others about my girls, I found these activities to be helpful expressions of mourning. To satisfy the longing for my girls, I watched home videos we had taken over the years, plus the recent ones Krista had filmed with her new video camera. The smile it brought to my face was like a warm massage to my heart.

I listened to my kids on the cassette tapes we had recorded. Just hearing them sing and recite their songs and lines from yearly Christmas programs was like having a fresh encounter with each of them. The same thing happened each time I uncovered a photo I hadn't seen before. I soon discovered something that many parents who lose children realize. I did not want anybody to forget my girls. I wanted the whole world to remember them. I have found that it's needful for a parent to keep the memory of their children alive.

I duplicated audiocassettes and made copies of poems and songs they had written, artwork they had made, and pictures that captured their personalities. I made videos from old movies and pictures of the girls with key people in their lives, and gave a lot of these as gifts.

As I created, I took on, in a sense, some of the girls' unique creativity. I became the Energizer Bunny with these projects—all of which were therapeutic for me. It showed me that when our pain is so great, it can actually stir up desire to learn something new. When the girls were alive, they had to show me how to use a DVD player. Now I make videos. The energy my grief created was used to focus on something constructive.

The purpose behind making the pictures and videos and connecting with friends was not just my need for people to remember the girls, however. It was also my effort to bring hope and healing to others. I found that a big part of my healing came when I thought about others, and this was just one expression of that.

When Joey graduated from high school, I had established a tradition of making a photo album from birth through graduation. Joey and Krista had received theirs, and since I had started Nikki's before the accident, I decided to finish it. Two years later, I was done—at least with Nikki's. I then began what became a three-year project of making Jessica's. Hers became harder as I progressed, knowing that when I was done with hers, I'd be done. There would be no more pictures that had been taken of them.

I would need to let go. Fortunately, letting go did not mean wiping them out of my memory. Letting go meant creating a new relationship with them without their physical presence.

I needed to keep their memory in a special place in my heart and mind, where they would always be—and where they remained vivid and real.

I often remembered the girls all at once because so many memories included us at times when we were together. But then I felt like I was robbing myself of the unique relationship I had with each daughter. Although not intentionally, I began experiencing "Krista," "Nikki," and "Jessica" days.

I felt much better as I dwelled on the lives they lived, rather than the fact that they were gone. I realized I was preparing myself to go forward by focusing on life versus death. Knowing that love endures forever, I trained myself to remember that they were still a part of my future because I would always carry them in my heart here on earth, and they would always be part of my eternity in heaven.

One of the ways I did this was through Krista's video camera. For a while, I took it everywhere and captured people and events I thought she would enjoy. I had so much fun doing it, and it made me feel as if I were seeing the world through her eyes. I went places I knew the girls enjoyed and took photos I thought they would take.

For the first few years, I occasionally wore their clothes—special T-shirts, jeans, and jewelry. I adopted some of their sayings like "Sweet!" and "Peace out!" I slept with Jess's blanket nearly every night for ten years, until it began to fall apart.

Most of all, I became more aware of how I treated people. I used to teach the girls godly character, but now I was learning from them as I heard testimonies of how they had treated people and viewed material possessions. Temporal things meant less and less to me. Now, as the girls stood in the presence of God, I saw them cheering me on to have eternal perspective and be Christ-like.

For the first four years, I loved having quiet time in my backyard each day, as I had done before they died, enjoying the flowers and watching the birds. This place was a sanctuary for me. After receiving many garden ornaments from friends and family, I spent hours in my garden tending it and decorating it with dragonflies to represent Krista, butterflies for Jessica, and turtles for Nikki. She also loved birds of any kind.

God met me in my garden many times to encourage me with symbols and representations of His love. I treasured special moments when a hummingbird perched on a nearby flower to watch me water the plants. To me, this meant Nikki wanted to be near me. A dragonfly would hover close by as a sign of Krista's love, or butterflies would often land on my arm or shoulder, greeting me with a kiss from Jessica.

I planted three miniature rose bushes I received as a gift; Krista's was red, Nikki's yellow, and Jess's pink. Nikki, usually the quiet one, never drew attention to herself and perhaps had wondered if anyone noticed her. While watching the rose bushes grow and bloom, I noticed that Nikki's bush was the most prolific, sweet with fragrance, and overflowing with vivid blossoms—a picture to me of her inner beauty that continues to blossom throughout eternity.

This was all very therapeutic, but I so missed the private jokes between my girls and me, and the little things they teased me about that wouldn't really be funny coming from anyone else—the funny stories, endearing moments, or reactions to awkward situations about which we often reminisced. These familiarities tell us we're a part of an intimate story of where, and with whom, we belong.

Because my world had become so sad, I craved laughter. At times I'd remind myself, *Lighten up, girl!* George MacDonald, the Scottish author and minister, said it well: "It is the heart that is not yet sure of God that is afraid to laugh in His presence."[5] So I launched myself on a mission to laugh. Not that I could force it, but I definitely prayed and watched for it.

One day at church, someone came up to me, laughing, and reminded me of when I had once walked into the glass doors there. I thought only Nikki, Jess, and I had experienced that hilarious scene. My untimely collision with the perfectly cleaned doors happened as

I entered for their first youth group meeting. I bounced backward a couple feet and fell on the outside steps, crying and holding my sore head. The girls laughed so hard they cried, which of course turned my tears into laughter.

Yet here was a young woman who had observed the mishap, telling me she had thought we would be fun to get to know because of our lightheartedness. Her words flooded me with warmth, knowing that someone else had shared our crazy experience. Parts of our personalities are downright laughable, and I have learned that if we take ourselves too seriously, we allow the enemy to rob us of some of the best medicine God has to offer.

One day years earlier, Krista waited for me in her car. As I approached her, she laughed hysterically. Finally, she managed to say, "Mom, look in the mirror!" One of the dark lenses from my sunglasses had fallen out. It really did look funny. But funnier yet was that I was absolutely clueless about it.

Fast-forward to a time while I was recording my CD. I felt especially sad when mixing one of the songs. It "rocked" (as Krista would say), and I knew she would have liked it. Sadder yet, it was her birthday. Then, squinting at the computer screen, I wondered why my vision was so blurry. Clueless again, the studio owner's wife came in and handed me the lens that had fallen out of my glasses. The coincidence on Krista's birthday became a funny gift and a beautiful healing memory, making it a "Krista" day.

You'd think that would have kept me smiling the whole way home. Instead, I felt sad all over again because the girls couldn't hear the song I'd recorded, and I started to cry. As soon as I drove onto the freeway, a billboard in front of me read, "Mom, you rock!" This was something Krista would have said, completing my "Krista" day with a huge smile.

While going through pictures, I came across one of Jessica, at eight or nine years old, on stage where Joey was playing a show. His guitar string broke and he asked if anyone in the audience had a joke to tell while he took time to fix it. Jessica eagerly took the stage to tell a joke about dog droppings. Everyone thought it was funny—except me.

It wasn't until I got over what the other adults thought that I could laugh about it. Seeing that picture set off a series of Jessica jokes, turning it into a "Jessica" day.

When Nikki was in kindergarten, we needed to buy her first set of glasses. She started to cry while we were in the store because she didn't want them. I brought her down to the lake for a walk and little pep talk. I have no idea what I said to her but it worked and, from then on, she was excited to wear glasses. Years later, Nikki came with me to buy my first pair of much-dreaded glasses. While trying them on, I didn't like how they looked on me. Nikki looked at me and playfully said, "Mom, do we need to take a little walk by the lake?"

Fast-forward to a recent time. I needed new glasses again. Not very happy about the selections, Nikki's words came to mind: *Do we need to take a walk by the lake?* That was a "Nikki" day.

One day while walking the familiar streets of my neighborhood where the girls so often walked, I envisioned their smiling faces. For a moment, I feared I might forget treasured memories with them. I then recalled the words of Peter Marshall from a book I was reading at the time: "Those we love are with the Lord, and the Lord has promised to be with us. If they are with Him, and He is with us, they can't be far away."[6]

Here is a section of the song I wrote about this, titled "I Can Still See Your Face."

I can still see your face; the memories will never be
Erased from the pictures of my mind.
They'll be treasures until time passes away, and I see your face again.
I can still see you smile as I recall the laughter for a while.
Each embrace that I hold dear for now I'll kiss you with my tears.
Until the day I see your face again.
When I fly away where everything will be made new
I'll be right there next to you when I'm finally home!
But while I wait, I will hold you in my heart.
If you're with God and God's with us, then we can't be far apart.

On my fiftieth birthday, the year after the girls died, Joe gave me a "letter from the girls" he wrote and read aloud at a surprise party for me. His own tears and emotion added to the impact it made. Although it was hypothetical, I believe it would have sounded something like this:

Happy Birthday, Mom

Happy birthday, Mom! It was not long ago that we thought fifty years was getting old. Well now, we have met people 1050, 2050, 3050, and older. Just like you, they are quite good looking for their age.

Remember on family vacations as we would drive, you would say, "Look how pretty this is, you guys." Or how you appreciated good things and said how beautiful they were? Heaven is so beautiful and incomprehensible that earthly words cannot describe its wonder. So we send to you that which you hold most dear. We send to you our love. Our heavenly Father sends His love also, along with our Lord and Savior, Jesus. Mom, you should hear the things they say about you. Human words are not enough. So for now, we'll tell you that they love you so much and are happy to have you in their family.

When you get to heaven, Mom, we will be there to greet you. We would introduce you to Jesus, but there is no mistaking Him in the crowd. Besides, He is always the first to greet and hug you.

You will always be our mom, because God gave moms to show children His love, and love never fails. But you will never have to care for us, for there is not a care here to care for. Believe us, Mom, that is far better. Better and better is a good way to describe heaven. For each day we see more of God's infinite heart of love. As the hymn says, "When you have been here ten thousand years" plus your fifty years, "you'll have no less days to sing God's praise than when you'd first begun." (Or something like that.)

In our Father's and Jesus' eternal love,

Krista, Nikki, and Jessica

God is my connection to my girls and my memories of them.

136

Chapter 17

Memorials to God's Power and Presence

Memories are the key not to the past,
but to the future.

—CORRIE TEN BOOM

Standing in my family room, aching for heaven, I sang a worship song by Sara Groves. Somehow, I sensed I had penetrated the veil between heaven and earth, and that my words joined with my girls' words, touching the heart of Jesus. Worshiping with them, I continued. This profound moment made me aware once again how thin the veil is. At that moment, I felt the undeniable presence of Jesus in my family room.

The girls and I had been great fans of Sara, and we had often sung her songs in the car and at home. A few months after my experience in the family room, Joe and I were at a local Christian book store where Sara was doing a signing for her new CD. We introduced ourselves, and I shared the testimony of my family room encounter. I told her how the girls and I had practiced that same song to sing at church and, although we never did get to sing it, I believed they were singing something like it now, only directly to Him.

That began a theme of worship for me—the idea of heaven and earth worshiping simultaneously, just in different realms. It also became the theme for our first memorial concert: "Praise the Lord from the heavens. ... Praise the Lord from the earth!" (Psalm 148:1, 7).

Our first memorial concert took place on January 1, 2005. The goal was to worship Jesus together from earth, along with all of heaven, as we remembered our girls and testified about God's faithful comfort.

Around the same time, we received a phone call from Don Moen, the worship leader of the *I Worship* Tour, a group of contemporary Christian musicians and singers who performed concerts together. He had read our story in *Charisma* magazine and gave us tickets to the concert and an invitation backstage. Sara, being a part of the tour, dedicated and sang "Jesus, You're Beautiful" to us, and "Great is Thy Faithfulness." She had no idea we had sung the traditional version at the girls' funeral, and that Joey and Bree had her version sung at their wedding. There was not one dry eye among the four of us.

Shortly after, we attended a recognition banquet given by the American Red Cross to honor those who had donated human organs that year. They invited each family to make a square for a quilt. When all the squares were sewn together, it would represent that year's donors. I dreaded it. But I made the square and attended the banquet with Joe, my sister and her daughters, my brother and sister-in-law, and one of the girls' close friends.

At the banquet, my sister grabbed a form to fill in with my daughters' favorite recipes for a Red Cross Cookbook they'd publish in honor of the donors. The thought of it seemed morbid to me, but I was told what a nice legacy from the girls it would be. I figured it would be selfish of me not to participate, so I took the form home.

I would have rather been making Christmas cookies with my girls than looking for their favorite recipes to put in a cookbook in memory of their deaths. Facing the task, I sat there and, instead, opened our mail only to find three letters from parents who had also lost their children to death, along with an invitation to a Christmas memorial service at the cemetery.

That did me in.

I swiped my hand over the tabletop and pushed every recipe, letter, and invitation to the floor. I didn't want to do any of these things! I did not want to read about one more dead child. I did not want to grieve. Period. I wanted to shop and make Christmas cookies—and be silly with my girls.

After my anger subsided, I read each letter more closely.

One of them contained a beautifully designed memorial program and a compassionate letter from two families that had experienced tragic accidents just days apart. Each family had lost a young son, and they were having a one-year memorial service for the two boys. I was deeply touched as I read the program and became vicariously acquainted with these two sweet boys who had probably met my girls by then. As I read about the deep faith these two families displayed, I felt encouraged by their expressed desire to glorify God. I awakened to an opportunity—to express my faith in and to God and honor my girls by creating a handout like theirs for our upcoming memorial service.

In spite of the icy weather that day, we had a big turnout for the service and, once again, heaven met earth and God was glorified. Local news stations covered it and openly reported on our eternal perspective.

For the second-year memorial service, we invited Sara Groves to join us with some other local musicians and friends. Bree and I had the honor and pleasure of singing "Jesus, You're Beautiful" with Sara, and I believe we were joined by the girls as we sang our love song to Jesus. A special connection was felt as Sara honored our girls and the Lord Jesus Christ in the songs she sang.

For the third-year anniversary, we had a quiet time at home, remembering the girls while I took a break from recording the CD. The fourth-year anniversary was celebrated by the release of my CD, with a memorial concert during which many people heard the message of eternal life.

Singing and worshiping at all these services brought a profound embrace between heaven and earth, time and eternity—and sorrow and joy. Such paradox.

Within the first four years, three documentaries were made of our story. My brother's church in Missouri produced the first one. After coming to Minnesota and hearing our story, they flew us and other family members there to share our story at two different Sunday services where the documentary was presented.

An evangelical broadcasting company in the Netherlands, called the EO, wanted to produce another documentary about us. They had become familiar with our story from the *Charisma* magazine article. They flew a crew from Holland to spend a week with us in our home, at our church, and with our friends. We filmed, cried, laughed, and worshiped God with them. The next year they flew us to Europe, where we had an opportunity to speak at churches in both Holland and France.

Many people were touched whenever the story was aired in Holland, Belgium, and Germany. It was also made available on the internet.

Days of Discovery from Grand Rapids, Michigan, produced the last documentary. Their crew also spent a week with us, and with the Backstrom family, who lost their three sons in a car accident nine months after our girls' death. A mutual friend introduced us, and our broken hearts were immediately joined, initiating us into an exclusive club of mourners—one we did not sign up for. In the years to follow, we met many other parents whose grief journeys were similar to ours, and yet we walked them out differently because no two grief journeys are alike.

The October before the accident, Joe and I had taken a trip with our girls to Florida. We planned our family vacation, figuring it would be the last trip we'd spend together, at least for a while, because the kids were getting older and Joey would soon be married. As it happened, Joey stayed home to work during that time before his wedding. We missed him but had a fabulous time making memories with the girls.

Five years after the girls died, we brought Joey and Bree to the same place. Like stepping back in time, our rooms were right off the volleyball court where I had once envisioned volleyball games with our growing family. After seeing it, Joey said, "That would be fun!" But then we all looked at one another, realizing it wouldn't be much of a game. Having Joey and Bree with us was a bittersweet reminder of the absence of the rest of our family. I was reminded of the precious time with the girls there, but I intentionally tried to seize opportunities to make new memories with Joey and Bree. While walking by familiar landmarks and recalling fun memories, I felt melancholy at the thought of leaving, as if I were saying goodbye to my girls all over again.

Joe wanted to do a fifth memorial service that year, and brought it up several times during the vacation, only to hear me say, "I can't do it." It was just too draining. I was burned-out from big-to-do events. I wanted life to be normal. I was tired of being the mother who lost three children.

Taking one last photo, I examined the landscaping stones that wound around the path of the resort's exit and sensed an impression from the Lord that silently spoke the words *memorial stones.*

God showed me that memorial stones are an important step in moving forward. Their purpose is to remember what God has done in and through our stories. The idea is similar to paging through a spiritual photo album to remember God's presence throughout. As a result, Joe and I left the resort discussing plans for the next memorial service. We decided to publicly celebrate Joey and Bree's fifth wedding anniversary at the same time we would remember the girls. After getting back home, I decided to find out a little more about memorial stones.

In Joshua 1, I read that Moses had died, and I'm sure Joshua was overwhelmed because of his death, but God called Joshua to go forward, promising to lead him into the promised land. By Joshua 3:8, the people had come to the edge of the Jordan River, and God told them to cross it. The river was normally about forty feet wide at its widest place. At that time, however, the river was much wider and at flood stage with a raging current. To step into the forceful water required courage and trust in God.

When I read this, God reminded me that He knew how hard it was for me to move forward because the waters of my sorrow were still at flood stage; even so, it was a perfect time for Him to show His power, and for me to trust Him. God stopped the Jordan's raging flow for thirty miles so the people could safely cross to the other side. Similarly, as Joe and I stepped into our river of sorrow, God promised to bring us across as well.

Joshua 4 describes how Joshua and the priests reached the other side of the Jordan and obeyed God's command to takes stones from the middle of the riverbed and pile them up on dry land as a memorial for what God had done for them. He wanted future generations to know about His faithfulness.

The Hebrew word for *memorial* means "to remember." Joshua, the priests, and the people remembered ceremoniously what God had done. This confirmed to me that we were to "remember with others" all the things God had done and that I was to continue to proclaim His faithfulness. As Psalm 40:9–10 says, "I proclaim your saving acts in the great assembly; I do not seal my lips, LORD, as you know. I do not hide your righteousness in my heart; I speak of your faithfulness and your saving help. I do not conceal your love and your faithfulness from the great assembly."

God reassured me He had been in the struggles with me while raising my kids, and He was with me in my present struggles, continuing to lead me forward: "As I was with Moses, so I will be with you; I will never leave you or forsake you" (Joshua 1:5). I also realized that if I wasn't paralyzing myself with memories of losing my girls, I was idealizing other memories through rose-tinted glasses. Either way it froze me in time, but God was calling me to engage in real life.

Going forward included remembering how He had moved in the girls' individual lives and ours as a family. This helped me see how my story fit into the bigger story of life, the story of God's redemption.

Corrie ten Boom exemplified this when she said, "Memories are the key not to the past, but to the future."[7]

I'm sure it was difficult for her to remember being separated from her elderly father, being imprisoned in a Nazi concentration camp, and watching her sister die. Yet, as she remembered God's faithful presence with her, she moved into a long future of ministering God's comfort and bringing hope to many.

Healthy remembering allows us to enjoy the life and memories we had with someone while treasuring all that God led us through. Remembering His faithful presence is what has motivated me to embrace the future that is to come, both for now and eternity.

Chapter 18

Strength
In Weakness

I simply think God is greater than our weakness.
In fact, I think it is our weakness that reveals how great God is.

—MAX LUCADO

The gift of memories brought comfort and encouragement to me as I traced God's faithfulness. But nothing could take the place of entering into my pain. I read that the only way to lessen pain was to move toward it, not away from it. Wounds don't simply go away by ignoring them; they need attention and care. There was no way of avoiding my grief. I had to embrace it. When the memorial services ended, the pictures were put away, and the videos were turned off, I was all alone—and the agonizing quietness of our house would scream.

Loss exposes our vulnerability, reminding us that we are not in control. It reveals our loneliness, our insecurities, and our unfulfilled longings. Loss shows us how weak we really are. I was weak all right, but according to 2 Corinthians 12:10, my weakness is what actually opens me up to God's power.

Psalms showed me how David confronted his limitations, called out to God, and begged for help. Overwhelmed, he pleaded with God to hear his cry, and he acknowledged that his heart felt faint. He asked

God to lead him to the rock that was higher than him (Psalm 61:1–3). When he despaired and felt abandoned, he questioned God about how long he would wrestle with his thoughts and sorrow (Psalm 13). But by the time he was done pouring out his heart to God in each of his psalms, he acknowledged that his hope, comfort, and victory were found in God alone.

This encouraged me to be honest with God and gave me permission to be weak. After all, David was called "a man after God's own heart," and this was not because he was strong in his flesh, that's for sure. David knew his own frame and where to go for help.

The Bible says that God has compassion on those who fear Him, just as a father has compassion on his children. He made us from dust to depend on Him as children depend on their father. Psalm 34:18 says, "The Lord is close to the brokenhearted and saves those who are crushed in spirit." I knew God lovingly longed to bring strength and comfort to me because that's who He is. Isaiah 61 tells me that He heals my broken heart and comforts me, gives me a crown of beauty for my ashes, the oil of joy for my sadness, and a garment of praise instead of my spirit of despair. It says He will call me an oak of righteousness, a planting for the display of His splendor.

To appreciate being likened to an oak tree, it helped to know a little about them. I discovered that at the beginning of an oak's life, the acorn's energy is first spent developing a root system before it sprouts anything above ground. That root system can spread four to seven times wider than the tree itself, which serves as a type of anchor during the worst of storms, allowing it to survive.

God reminded me over and over that He calls me an oak of righteousness. He does the planting, which takes the pressure off me. His foundation of love has been growing since my first encounter with Him and goes deeper than any trouble that ever touches me.

About three years before the accident, Nikki recited a narration at a church Christmas program. It spoke of the gospel as being a love story, and how in the hearing of it—if we really listen—we begin to see who we really are as God's beloved.

Even though our circumstances had inconceivably changed since she read that, the truth of what she read that night has not wavered. Jesus Christ is the same yesterday, today, and forever. His love is never-ending. It's eternal.

A friend of ours pointed out something that has brought great comfort at some of our weakest moments. Hebrews 11:4 says that because of Abel's sacrifice to God, he was commended as righteous and he continues to speak even though he is dead. He pointed out that Nikki also continues to speak, though she is dead. All three of the girls do—not because of any profound or extraordinary feats. Just simple expressions of loving God and others have left enduring marks on people's lives, and continue to do so. The same is true for all of us.

Abel died young, and we might conclude that his life was wasted, cut short, and didn't accomplish much. Cain, on the other hand, whose sacrifice did not please God because it was not done in faith, lived a long life. But Abel is the one mentioned in the heroes-of-the-faith list, not Cain. Telling our story carries great sadness because the girls were so young, yet it resonates great eternal joy because they continue to speak of God's love.

Almost immediately after the accident, God launched us into a ministry of sharing our story through radio, newspaper, television, neighbors, schools, and churches. We even shared at a punk rock concert that paid tribute to the girls. Other than the memorial services, we didn't initiate one speaking engagement. For nearly six years I was invited to speak at least twice a month, and, for a shorter period, nearly three out of four weekends.

I knew our story was something far bigger than me. I felt a bit like Dorothy in *The Wizard of Oz*. I was in a frightening, unfamiliar place, but at the same time, I felt excited to meet new people wherever we went. Like Dorothy, I knew an enemy was out to destroy me. I could picture myself with eyes shut, clicking my heels together, and reciting, "There's no place like home, there's no place like home," hoping to wake up and find myself safely back to the way things had been. But it was no dream, and I was indeed weak compared to the task ahead of me. I sometimes felt like a sought-after actor in a movie, but inadequate for the role. When people invited me to share my story, I felt unqualified. A nobody really. Just Debbie, the mom.

One day while thinking about how unqualified I was, the Holy Spirit reminded me of the verse I memorized with the youth group for a mission trip the year before: "When I came to you, I did not come with eloquence or human wisdom as I proclaimed to you the testimony about God. For I resolved to know nothing while I was with you except Jesus Christ and Him crucified. I came to you in weakness with great fear and trembling. My message and my preaching were not with wise and persuasive words, but with a demonstration of the Spirit's power, so that your faith might not rest on human wisdom, but on God's power" (1 Corinthians 2:1–5).

I knew full well it wasn't because of my speaking expertise that I was to tell our story. It was because of who He was and all He did through our story. That's not to say I didn't need to prepare. I did. To prepare, I spent time with God and depended on His strength as He displayed His splendor through me.

Paul tells us we are earthen vessels, jars of clay that contain heavenly treasures. *The Message* puts it this way: "If you only look at us, you might well miss the brightness. We carry this precious Message around in the unadorned clay pots of our ordinary lives. That's to prevent anyone from confusing God's incomparable power with us" (2 Corinthians 4:7 MSG). One day, while driving in the car and dwelling on my insecurities, a voice on the radio said matter-of-factly and confidently, "God loves to use cracked pots." Well, I fit the analogy.

The story of Gideon illustrates this well. In Judges 7, God gave Gideon the strange orders to position his army around the Midian camp with trumpets and clay pots containing torches. When Gideon signaled, each soldier blew his trumpet and broke his jar. The noise from the trumpets and fires from the pots caused panic, and the Midianites killed each other in confusion.

A pot in those days was practically designed to hold something, not to be an object of beauty alone. Attention wasn't drawn to the pot, but to what was inside. I realized I am like a pot of clay, an earthen vessel, designed to shine God's light in the darkness of my circumstances. I am meant to display "the light of the knowledge of the glory of God" (2 Corinthians 4:6), which God placed inside of me to show others that any power is from Him alone. I knew God wanted people to see His power in my life, but, more than that, He wanted me to see it because, of all people, I knew what I was made of.

Our last Christmas with the girls, when I bought Jessica *The Lord of the Rings* trilogy, I also purchased (more for myself than for her) *Finding God in The Lord of the Rings* by Kurt Bruner and Jim Ware. The little book of reflections points out truth and insights from the classic story applicable for our lives today. Even though Tolkien did not write *The Lord of the Rings* as an allegory of the gospel, his Christian worldview shows up throughout the books. After Jessica passed, I longed to connect with her as I read. God showed me truths through this little book—about myself, God, and my journey of grief.

As I continued to consider the verses in Corinthians about being clay pots carrying God's message, I felt like Frodo, just a simple hobbit from Middle Earth, not particularly qualified for the task set before him yet faced with no other choice. I began to see myself as being honored by God to be entrusted with my story, although that insight fluctuated as often as my feelings. For the most part, I felt chosen. Just as simple, ordinary hobbits had been chosen for a great purpose, so had I been chosen in this story of loss, and it was not because of my own strength or wisdom. I was encouraged that God uses weak, ordinary people to display His strength.

I have come to discover that the Christian walk is made up of a divine paradox because God's ways are higher than ours. Oftentimes joy can only come through sorrow. Jesus experienced this more than any of us—for the joy set before Him, He endured the cross.

Scripture speaks of the need to lose to gain, surrender to win, serve to rule, die to live, and give to receive. In this case, my weakness brought God's strength: "My grace is sufficient for you, for my power is made perfect in weakness" (2 Corinthians 12:9). In the hobbits' land of Middle Earth, they had their own proverbs, stories, and sayings of the wise, just as God's people do. Ours are written in God's Word.

The hobbits knew not to look within themselves for wisdom or hidden knowledge but to look at what had been already revealed in times past. I also could not draw on my own ideas and thoughts for wisdom and strength. I needed to know God's Word and depend on what He has already revealed. I am not equipped or strengthened *in spite* of my weaknesses, but *because* of them. If I allow my weaknesses to open me to God's power, I become strong in Him.

In 2 Corinthians 1:8, Paul wrote of being under great distress in Asia, so far beyond his ability to endure that he despaired even of life itself. He could not rely on himself but on God, who raises the dead. Paul spoke enthusiastically about God's strength to deliver him in his time of great weakness. "He *has delivered* us from such a deadly peril, and he *will deliver* us again. On him we have set our hope that he will *continue to deliver* us" (2 Corinthians 1:10, emphasis mine). Paul shows how God covers every tense. God's strength is in the past, present, and future.

I cannot help but see God's display of strength *because* of our tragedy. Second Corinthians 12:9 says God's strength is made perfect in our weakness. The Greek word for *perfect* primarily means "complete." Therefore, when I am weak in myself, I am indeed strong in Him.

People have come up with sayings that actually bring on more pain and confusion than healing. One of the most quoted to me was, "God will never give you more than you can handle." Not true. Where is that in the Bible? I knew I couldn't handle all this pain. I desperately needed God's help, but despite knowing this, I still felt condemned when someone said those words to me. Then one day I heard someone else say that God often allows us to experience more than we can handle so we will depend on Him. That rang true and liberated me.

The apostle Paul even wrote that he was under more distress than he was able to bear. My grief and sorrow were also much more than I could bear. I needed God. His power works best in our weakness. In fact, He doesn't work at all in our self-sufficiency; that only prolongs our struggle. We cannot receive His strength until we realize we have none. His strength only works in realized weakness. The truth is, my weakness is the key to intimacy with Him and dependency on Him—unreservedly so.

Chapter 19

Green Pastures
and Still Waters

In the course of time I came to realize that nothing so quieted
and reassured the sheep as to see me in the field.
The presence of their master, owner and protector put
them at ease as nothing else could.

—*A SHEPHERD LOOKS AT PSALM 23* BY PHILIP KELLER

One of the many books given to us about grief stated that a rea-
sonable amount of time to work through loss was one to three
years. Somewhere in my tangled thinking, I figured, since I was grieving for three people, it would take me nine years. But after meeting
many members in this new club of mourners, I discovered it takes a
lifetime.

Each person experiences the grief process in their own time and
way. After several years, I was still on the first leg of my journey. The
tragic loss of my daughters seemed to be always in the present. Never
did it seem to be in the past. This unchanging reality was far beyond
my ability to control.

I process and understand truth in my life most often through
word pictures and analogies. One of my favorite books is the time-
less allegory *Hinds' Feet on High Places* by Hannah Hurnard. I had
always identified with the main character, a cowering girl named

Much-Afraid. Deformities on her face and feet caused her to talk with a stutter and walk with a limp, representing her many fears and insecurities. Much-Afraid struggles to be free and whole as she follows the Chief Shepherd to the High Places, where he has promised to give her hinds' feet, enabling her to ascend even higher to the Peaks. As she journeys to the High Places, she sees the world from a new perspective—through the eyes of love.

In the end she is transformed into a beautiful, victorious soul; however, early on in her upward climb, the Shepherd gives her two dreaded companions, whose names are Sorrow and Suffering, to accompany her on her perilous journey. Like Much-Afraid, Sorrow and Suffering had become my companions, as they do for so many traveling to the high places. When the Shepherd introduced them to me, I shouted fearfully along with Much-Afraid, "I can't go with them!"

But the Shepherd answered her, and me, in a kind voice: "Fear not … only believe. I promise that you shall not be put to shame. Go with Sorrow and Suffering, and if you cannot welcome them now, when you come to the difficult places where you cannot manage alone, put your hand in theirs confidently and they will take you exactly where I want you to go."[8]

I slowly learned to put my hand in theirs. If I wanted to rise above my present place to the higher ground of healing, I would have to climb steep slopes and embrace my pain. At times, I wondered how I could scale the intimidating mountains in front of me. Other times I felt I was moving toward the mountain peaks, when suddenly my thoughts and feelings took me on a detour through a desert. As I walked through these lonely places, I learned many things about depending on my Shepherd.

I related to Much-Afraid while meeting countless obstacles and seemingly impossible situations along the way, realizing that for some strange reason they were permitted by the Shepherd. Just like Much-Afraid, I felt tempted at times to end my quest for love and healing because of threatening encounters with fear, pride, resentment, bitterness, self-pity, and despair.

The Good Shepherd reminded me again and again that He would bring to fruition the seed of love He had planted in my heart and He would lead me to a place of healing. He assured me that my undeserved loss would produce in me His beautiful character if I trusted in Him through each difficulty. In the end, Much-Afraid received a new name from the Shepherd. She became Grace and Glory and her companions changed from Sorrow and Suffering to Peace and Joy.

One Saturday morning, Joe and I sat on the sunny patio of a nearby coffee shop, and while sipping our favorite coffee drinks, began a study on the Twenty-Third Psalm. Two key truths stood out to me.

The first was from verse two: "He makes me lie down in green pastures and leads me beside still waters." When I think of green pastures, I think of the lush green hillsides and grasslands of southern Minnesota. I envisioned the sheep of this psalm lying comfy in the soft green grass. But after doing a little research, I learned that these types of green pastures don't exist in Israel. Sheep graze on dry, rocky hillsides with hardly any vegetation. Grass grows in small tufts and clumps that sprout up around rocks and in cracks and crevices. The sheep are completely dependent on the shepherd to lead them to the food and rest they need.

This gave me a clearer picture because the landscape of my life felt more like a rocky desert than green hillsides. I needed to get on with life—to green pastures—and, although it took a long time, I discovered that getting on with life is not abandoning my old life and current pain. I somehow needed to bring all of it into my new normal. Only the Good Shepherd could lead me to the green pastures I needed.

The second truth was that sheep are easily frightened and will not drink from turbulent waters. They depend on their shepherd to lead them to calm water. The waters of my circumstances were too turbulent for me to drink from. I could barely read my Bible for a while. Although I always believed in God's Word and wanted to read it, there were times when I just could not concentrate.

God led me beside still waters. My gentle places to drink were cards that people sent to us with spiritual messages and Scriptures inside; music and songs I listened to; the girls' journals I often read; and dreams, that felt so real and let me see and be with my girls. Still waters are unique to everyone, and these were mine.

Once I showed a friend the picture boards of the girls because she was unable to attend the funeral. While looking at their photographs, a painful desire rose up in me. I wanted so much to touch and hug each of them again.

With my heart aching, I went to bed that night and dreamed about them. The experience met my deep need. In reflection, I realized how often God spoke to me through dreams from the time I first came to Jesus. In my dream, Krista entered the room and ran up to me. We exchanged a long embrace. I touched her. The experience felt exceptionally real. Our eyes locked and then with a radiant smile she said, "Mom, we love you and we miss you, but I have to go now!"

I woke up energized for my day as if I had just spoken with all three of them. It somehow motivated me to go through some of their remaining personal belongings.

Another night, after crying for some time, I dreamed I was lying on the floor, weeping. Krista knelt beside me, placing her hands on me, and began praying, "Oh Jesus, comfort my mom." Again, I woke up with peace, reminded of the fact Jesus Himself is praying for me (Romans 8:34).

Still waters.

Soon after, I dreamed about Jessica and then Nikki. In both dreams I looked into their eyes, and they radiated comfort and encouragement to me—to do the "thing in front of me." These dreams, and many more, have been still waters, bringing comfort and peace to me because they represent love that endures. Love never fails.

Dreams are a common experience in grief and, for me, they were God's kind and timely gifts. But the Word of God is what brought me lasting healing. For nourishment, the Good Shepherd leads His sheep to green pastures and, still waters for nourishment, refreshment, and rest. It is there we receive refreshment and peace, cleansing, and healing. Jesus is my gentle Shepherd who knows me intimately and cares for me.

My relationship with God has deepened and developed throughout my journey, giving me a sense of security. Although this did not exempt me from devastations of the storm, it has empowered and equipped me to go through the pain of grief because of the core foundational truths He had already established early on.

One night, while feeling sad and alone, unable to sleep and unable to read, I wondered for a bit if God even cared. Just as sheep cannot not lie down or keep quiet if they are hungry or afraid, so it was with me. My pasture seemed anything but green, and my waters of grief were anything but still. I needed to know God was present. I longed for His comfort and cried out to Him.

In the next moment, I believe it was God who urged me to get up and look at the sympathy cards tucked away in Jessica's room. Acting on the prompting, I got out of bed and looked through a boxful of cards. Tears washed down my tired face as I pulled out card after card. At last, while opening one of the last ones, a small card with a Scripture landed softly on my lap. On it was a picture, a sculpture of a hand with a child resting in the hand's palm. The words on the card were from Isaiah 49:15. In that moment, God gently reminded me, "See, I will not forget you. I have carved you in the palm of my hand."

God spoke to me through the image on the card and its Scriptures, just as He had done in the past through His Word, reminding me, like a flood, about so many of His promises: He will never leave me nor forsake me; I belong to Him; He carries me and will never let me go; I am His bride and He's preparing a place for me. That night I jotted down words that resulted in a song titled "You are Mine."

I will hold you in the palm of My hand.
I will carry you through this lonely wilder-land.

I will whisper words of comfort in your ear;
Reminding you, My child, there's nothing to fear.
I will never leave you. I will not forsake you.
I'll never let you out of my sight.
I will not forget you. My love is always for you.
I've carved you in the palm of My hand.
I will love you with an everlasting love.
Until I take you home to your mansion up above.
I will be with you till the end of all time.
I love you, child; I have called you Mine.
In the darkest of nights, when I seem out of sight,
My truth is the light to guide you here.
When you feel all alone and you're longing for home,
just rest in My arms
And know I'm always here.
You are Mine; I've carved you in the palm of My hands.

One of many mornings of feeling overwhelmed and weak, desperate to hear from God, I picked up one of my favorite devotional books, hoping for relief for my still raw emotions. It quoted Luke 18:1 about how men ought always to pray, and ended saying that to faint is to fail. God's voice seemed distant and I felt faint in every way—too faint to even pray. Those words ironically triggered feelings of failure. What help I'd hope to find became rough and turbulent waters.

However, my gentle Shepherd led me to still waters. After closing that book, I picked up *My Utmost for His Highest* by Oswald Chambers, and opened to the devotional reading for May 8th. As I read, my soul drank from a cool, refreshing stream: "You cannot see Him just now, you cannot understand Him or what He is doing, but you know *Him*. Shipwreck occurs when there is not the mental poise which comes from being established on the eternal truth that God is Holy *Love*."[9]

There it was—my truth: God's love. The most powerful force in the universe. Love is the greatest motivator. He first loves me, and

156

I cannot help but to respond. The truth is that God loved me long before I chose to return His love. His love drew me to Him when I was living life my own way. It was His love that secured my eternity by hanging on a cross and taking my sins upon Himself. And it was His love that brought me through many smaller storms before the loss of my girls.

In that very moment when my mind and heart felt terribly frail, God took initiative—and met me with exactly what I needed. No grief is ever too big to separate us from the love of God. What a liberating and comforting truth it is to know that nothing can separate me from Him. Nothing—no, not a thing—can separate me from God.

I read more healing words from the same page: "I know your deeds. See, I have placed before you an open door that no one can shut. I know that you have little strength, yet you have kept my word and have not denied my name. I am coming soon. Hold on to what you have, so that no one will take your crown" (Revelation 3:8, 11). My Shepherd knew I was struggling in faith, and yet reaffirmed me regarding my relationship with Him.

Whenever God seemed distant, He'd remind me of His nearness. God really is the Good Shepherd, and not only did He speak my language and bring me to green pastures and still waters, but He continually brought me back to the beginning place in my relationship with Him: my need and His ever-present love.

Chapter 20

Walking Through the Shadowlands

Grief is like a long valley, a winding valley where
any bend may reveal a totally new landscape.
—*A Grief Observed* by C. S. Lewis

One minute I'd be resting in the green pastures of God's Word, peacefully drinking from the still waters of His Spirit, when suddenly my path would descend into the valley of the shadow of death. King David knew God was with him in this valley, and I believed God's presence was with me too: "Even though I walk through the valley of the shadow of death, I fear no evil, for You are with me" (Psalm 23:4 NASB).

Real geographical valleys of the shadow of death exist. A friend of mine visited Israel and told me these valleys are narrow paths with steep sides that descend from Jerusalem to Jericho and along the western side of the Dead Sea. These areas are considered dangerous places to travel through. The shadows grow dangerously dark due to the cliffs that block the sun, and they hide turns in the path. This makes opportune places for thieves and wild animals to lie in wait for their victims.

As I journeyed in faith, the darkness of my grief made me vulnerable to the attacks of the enemy. God's enemy and mine looked for opportune moments to attack me, just as it is written: "The thief comes only to steal and kill and destroy; I have come that they may have life, and have it to the full" (John 10:10). I consistently fended off discouragement, fear, and despair. One day, however, God reminded me of a dream He had given me about a year before the girls died.

In my dream, I was walking down the street, and in the sky the clouds took on the form of three sinister demons focusing on me. They cupped their hands to their mouth while threatening me with these words: "Bow down to us or we will destroy you!" Trying to intimidate me, the spokes-demon (of unbelief), who seemed the essence of all three, said again, "You must bow down to us or we will kill you!"

I looked at the people around me for help, but they were oppressed and weighed down with heavy bundles, like backpacks, on their backs. Continuing to walk, I sang a song ever so quietly about bowing down to the One who gave His life for me. I was able to straighten my posture and continue singing.

My confidence increased and I sang with greater authority. My gait quickened into a battle march as I sang the song with boldness and lifted my hands in praise to the one true God. The demons dissipated, the backpacks fell from people's backs, and everyone, including me, began to worship God and walk about freely.

I awakened from the dream full of desire to praise and worship my God in defiance of the intimidating assaults of the enemy and my own depressed feelings, realizing my proclamation and praise was just as much for other people's freedom as my own.

As I remembered that dream, it helped me realize that walking through the valley is not unique to my life. We are all on a journey that takes us through this dark valley at some point. I realized this was God's reminder of just how much I need to praise the Lord to battle the intimidating enemies that threaten to destroy me. I saw the connection and importance of concern for others in navigating through my own valley. In response, I couldn't help but play my piano or guitar, sing worship songs to Jesus, and listen to praise music as I fell asleep at night. At the same time, I became even more motivated in my ministry of leading worship.

While I researched and read about sheep, I learned that they will run away if they are frightened, thus becoming even more vulnerable because they're unprotected. I struggled often against the desire to isolate myself and run from people. I finally chose to contend for the relationships that had been established in my life. I became intentional about staying connected to others. I understood and even experienced, at times, that isolation would make me an even easier prey to the dark voices of discouragement.

Since a shepherd has an intimate knowledge of each sheep in their flock, they call them by name and are familiar with each one's characteristics. The shepherd instinctively knows when one of their sheep is hurt.

I took courage from the verse in which Jesus said, "'My sheep listen to my voice. I know them, and they follow me. I give them eternal life, and they shall never perish; no one will snatch them out of my hand'" (John 10:27–28). I was safe in God's hands. I knew the voice of my Shepherd but, more importantly, I knew He knew me. He knows my name, my weaknesses, and my every need. He knows when something is wrong with me and takes extra care to call my name and lead me.

Even though sheep don't know why their shepherd leads them through dark, scary valleys (on the way to green pastures), they still follow him. They know the shepherd cares for their good. Although I wasn't sure where God was leading me, I felt safe in His presence.

As much as I wanted out of the shadowlands, I recognized my peace and safety did not depend on getting over my pain and out of my valley. I would never stop missing my girls; however, my peace came from the truth that my Shepherd was close to me and in control. He was my Sovereign God, and His love was trustworthy.

Joe often uses an example of when the kids were little. He would set them on a countertop or high platform and, like many fathers do, he would hold out his hands and encourage them to leap into his arms. "Jump!" he would call out. They never hesitated because they knew he would catch them; they trusted him. This picture of simple trust in their daddy is how we can be with God.

When Jessica was learning the ABCs of God in Sunday school, she came home proudly after church, declaring in her high, sweet five-year-old voice, "God is i-n-c-o-m-p-r-e-h-e-n-s-i-b-l-e! That means He is more than we can fully comprehend." Then she recited, "Who has known the mind of the Lord? Or who has been his counselor?" (Romans 11:34).

After that little Bible lesson from Jess, as situations arose in our lives that made no sense, Joe and I would look at each other and say, "Incomprehensible!"—our buzz word to trust God.

Incomprehensible!

Satan is powerful, but there are limits to his power. According to Job 1:10–12, Satan had power in Job's life, but only what God allowed. No evil or calamity can come to us unless allowed by the God of the universe. I believe God has eternal purposes we know nothing about concerning the things He allows in our lives.

In Job 38:4, God responded to Job's questions concerning His fairness and justice, but instead of answering Job's *why* questions, He asked Job a question: "Were you there when I laid the earth's foundations? Tell me if you understand." Like Job, I wasn't there either. How can I possibly begin to understand the eternal purposes of pain and suffering when I can't even comprehend how God set the world in motion?

In his book *Don't Waste Your Life*, John Piper wrote, "God made man small and the universe big to say something about Himself."[10] Who are we to challenge God's mind or presumptuously attempt to advise or question Him? But that is exactly what we do when we try to figure out why He allows what He does. Isaiah 55:9 tells us that God's thoughts and ways are higher than ours.

We cannot possibly begin to understand everything about God— but we can trust Him. If I cannot trust in God's sovereignty, then all I can conclude is that God is weak and something got by Him, or that He simply doesn't care. But I know that neither theory is true because He's proven His power and love over and over to me both experientially and through His Word. I can either bow down to unbelief and allow it to intimidate me and rob me of sensing God's presence and goodness, or I can live in the confidence that He loves me.

After praying for me, a friend gave these words to me from God: "Trust in the LORD with all your heart and lean not on your own understanding" (Proverbs 3:5). As I meditated on that Scripture, I discovered God does not instruct us to understand Him with all our heart; He tells us to *trust* Him with all our heart and not lean on our own understanding. I am also told to love Him with all my heart: "Love the LORD your God with all your heart and with all your soul and with all your strength" (Deuteronomy 6:5).

Our dog, Buddy, sure loved us, but only humans made in the image of God have a heart capable of loving God, which is exactly why the enemy of our soul tries to distort and stifle our love for God. I've heard it said, "It is not my ability, but my response to God's ability, that counts." My response-ability to God is to trust and love Him. I will never know all the answers or have all the explanations for things that happen on this side of heaven, but through God's revealed Word, I do know the character of His unfailing, unchanging, and unconditional love for me.

When a small child falls down, all he or she really needs is to be picked up by Daddy. A smile of reassurance and affirmation of love, and everything is all right. That's what God did for me. I am His little girl and He loves me. I did not need to understand my circumstances, but rather believe in His love for me. "See what great love the Father has lavished on us, that we should be called children of God" (1 John 3:1).

When I walked through the valley of the shadows, God showed me there is a difference between shadows and the real thing, recapping once again what He showed me the night the girls died. Walking through shadowlands is temporary, but dwelling with Him is forever. I may have to walk through the valley, but I certainly do not have to live there. I will dwell in the house of the Lord forever, and it begins now.

My girls are dead to this life but very alive in heaven, where there are no shadows and only light, living in a greater reality than I can imagine. I am the one living in the shadowlands, walking it out day by day in my humanness, dependent on my Shepherd for guidance.

Pastor, speaker, and author Tony Evans says, "Most people think we are in the land of the living on our way to the land of the dying. But actually, we are in the land of the dying on our way to the land of the living. That's why I say death is a conjunction, not a period. It is a bridge between this life and the life to come."[11]

What we really seek through our *why* questions is peace. More than answers, most of us just want a sense of closure with some restoration and sense of meaning. But even if one of my questions were answered, I would have endless others. Even if all of my *why* questions were answered, they would not bring back my girls. My peace does not come through understanding, but through trusting God. Although my understanding is limited, there are no limits to my trust in God.

Luke 1:78–79 tells me: "Through the heartfelt mercies of our God, God's Sunrise will break in upon us, shining on those in the darkness, those sitting in the shadow of death" (MSG). There must be a source of light to see a shadow. There is a shadow only because something is blocking the light. Death casts a shadow on life, but we have the Light of Life living in and with us. He is Jesus, the Light of the World, who walks in the valley with us.

Part Five

DARKNESS BEFORE DAWN

Chapter 21

Veiled Perspective

*Tears are not only telling you something about the secret
of who you are, but more often than not God is speaking
to you through them of the mystery of where you have
come from and is summoning you to where,
if your soul is to be saved, you should go to next.*

—Fredrick Buechner

I was so thankful that God's light was there to continue shining through the shadows in my life. Even after all He had showed me, I still struggled as my feelings would often scream at me that life was not okay. But I remembered the truths God had spoken and remained consciously aware that He was calling me forward. Integrating these truths to my life, however, was not easy. It took time. Lots of it.

As much as I wanted and expected to go forward, my feelings told me I could not. I felt like a crybaby. Tears seemed to be a way of life, almost my second language. When I was alone, the tiniest thing could set me off.

Around this time, my brother-in-law told me about a man who was recruiting helpers for an orphanage. When the babies first came to them at the children's home, they cried continually, but because the orphanage had a shortage of workers, the babies could not be attended to properly. Sadly, their unaided cries gradually ceased altogether.

It's good to remember that a healthy baby cries to communicate their discomfort or need. A baby's cry is also unique. Voice researchers call these unique sounds "cry prints," which are as individual as finger-prints. If unattended, a baby learns that his or her cries do nothing and the child will stop signaling, giving up hope for attention.

It was then that I realized my cries were actually a demonstration of hope, knowing God heard me. My tears, a sign of my humanity, reminded me of my need for God. I sensed God saying to me, "My child, you're not losing hope. You know that I hear your cries and will attend to them. I made you this way." He was holding me in His hand (Isaiah 41:10).

As I thought more about a crying baby, I realized that I had never expected my own crying babies to fix things for themselves. Joey went through a colicky stage as a baby, which is how I thought of myself now. He didn't have the ability to help himself, so I held him close to comfort him. God doesn't expect us to fix ourselves either. He doesn't shake His finger impatiently, shaming us to get our lives together and stop crying. He is compassionate and holds us close. He wants to comfort us like a mother comforts her nursing child (Isaiah 66:13).

In fact, because we have been nurtured and comforted by God, we become qualified to care for and comfort others.

As a young Christian, I heard a preacher teach about being "broken bread and poured-out wine" for others. His message gripped my heart and moved me to pray to be that for others. Romanticizing what that meant, I gave no thought to the breaking that happens before bread can be eaten, or the pruning and crushing process grapes go through to become poured-out wine.

I learned, early on in my walk with God, that in any spiritual journey we take, the process is the most important part. It's also the hardest part. It exposes us, showing us what we're made of, provid-ing for us opportunity to depend on God. This is where we can be conformed to the image of Christ. This is where we can partake of the fellowship of His sufferings (Philippians 3:10). That's also what qualifies us to feed and nourish others as we receive His comfort (2 Corinthians 1:3–5). But in order to receive His nurture and comfort, I had to realize it was His love that was doing the squeezing.

One day while reading my Oswald Chambers devotional, I read, "If we are ever going to be made into wine, we will have to be crushed; you cannot drink grapes. Grapes become wine only when they have been squeezed."[12] As I considered that, I recalled something my dad used to say when I was a little girl: "I'm going to squeeze the juice out of you," which was always followed by a big bear hug. Now I had a picture of God and me. He was lovingly squeezing the juice out me so I could be poured-out wine that would benefit His other children. When I realize it's His love, nourishment pours out. When I resist God's love, I become stifled and I dry up.

Living through pain knowing you're loved by God gives us credibility as people observe us. This motivated me to continue moving forward.

During one of my crying episodes, I opened my devotional to the Scripture I mentioned to the reporters the day after the girl's accident: "Unless a kernel of wheat falls to the ground and dies, it remains only a single seed. But if it dies, it produces many seeds" (John 12:24). Feeling broken, I was once again tempted to question the wisdom of God in allowing my girls to die. But while reading the devotional *Streams in the Desert*, I read October 15th's entry, called "Broken Things," and God once again spoke to my heart:

God uses most for His glory those people and things which are most perfectly broken. The sacrifices He accepts are broken and contrite hearts. It is when a beautiful grain of corn is broken up in the earth by DEATH, that it's inner heart sprouts forth and bears hundreds of other grains. And thus, on and on, through all of history, and all biography, and all vegetation, and all spiritual life, God must have BROKEN THINGS.[13]

Although broken, I was encouraged that my brokenness would result in being used to bring life.

There were times when I cried for joy over the love I sensed from my heavenly Father, recognizing how I was a part of something so wonderfully eternal and realizing I only saw a fraction of His purposes. God gave me an insightful illustration of that eternal perspective as I sat at my kitchen table one day, replaying the *why* questions.

My eyes caught sight of a gathering of ants on the floor. They were busy at work in their little corner of the room, and my thoughts drifted from how to get rid of them, to imagining their viewpoint of life. They scurried around in their little corner of the house, in their little corner of our neighborhood, in their little corner of New Brighton, Minnesota.

A couple of ants were being quite brave, adventurous enough to venture into the family room. It amazed me to think that ants are capable of lifting up to a hundred times their own body weight. I once read that if a second grader were relatively as strong as an ant, the child could lift up a car. Ants are indeed one of God's strongest creatures for their size. But the fact is, no matter how industrious or persistent any one of these ants were, it was likely that not one would make it out of the house. This was their world and all they would ever see and experience. Their view of the world was exceptionally limited compared to mine.

Although we are made in the image of God, we are still finite. How much grander is God's perspective compared to my puny view. These little ants reminded me that God sees the whole picture—one I cannot begin to fathom.

For some time, Joe talked about moving to a smaller house that required less upkeep. Four and a half years after the girls died, we finally made the decision to move. Our house sold, and we began our search for a new one. Nothing seemed good enough for me, but Joe felt confident and kept reassuring me that God had something good for us. I had two prerequisites: a walking trail close by and a backyard sanctuary. We finally found a townhouse we liked, and it bordered a lovely wooded area—with a deck that faced the trees and a walking trail nearby.

We had a month to pack. I knew moving was a big deal, but I was still caught off guard by the triggering of our loss all over again, which caused a lot of anxiety in me. Sorting through keepsakes and school projects in our basement storage room was saying goodbye to everything familiar. Again.

The mildew in our basement also brought on an allergic reaction, and I lost my voice for two weeks and soon had a hard time breathing. I finally went to the doctor and was told I was having panic attacks instead. That frightened me. Medicine helped a bit.

It especially helped to have Joe hold me. He was like Jesus with skin on. We'd put on worship music, read Scripture, and pray. After a while, the severity of the attacks subsided, but at times, I would still experience difficulty breathing and swallowing. Joe would tell me I was okay, and since I trusted him and I trusted God, I knew I would be all right.

Then moving day arrived. Now I was leaving the memory-filled rooms. Though the people were gone, the visuals had still been reminders of the family life that had once filled our home and my heart with joy. Now I was losing even that.

A new house—but not a home. At least not yet. It seemed cold. No memories. Nothing familiar. I felt depressed, weak, and unspiritual. *After all God has brought me through, why can't I be stronger?*

People told me that we would make new memories in our new home. I wanted to believe them, but half of the people I wanted to make memories with were gone. I tried to be patient.

The thing that attracted me to the townhouse was the deck's view of nature, the green space and trees. We intended to put a window in the living room to enjoy the beautiful view from inside, but we couldn't because of the townhouse association's property restrictions. I either had to go out on my deck or position a chair in front of the sliding glass door in my kitchen to see the view. The glass door became my way into Narnia. Each of us has our own method of recharging and getting ahold of God. One of mine has always been nature.

Sometimes I had to move things around a little or reposition myself to see what I needed. Oftentimes I had to go outside to have a completely different view. This happens on our spiritual journey as well. I have found that simply repositioning myself can help me connect with God. Other times I need to accept my limitations and believe He's there. We will often encounter obstacles that block our vision of God, and although circumstances, thoughts, or feelings may hinder our view, that does not change the fact that He's present.

I may not see, but the important thing to remember is that He sees everything. His view is infinitely greater than mine, like the analogy of the ants. He sees things that are out of our natural view because He sees the whole story from beginning to end. He is the author of the book of our life.

A. W. Tozer tells us in *The Pursuit of God*:

> A spiritual kingdom lies all about us, enclosing us, embracing us, altogether within reach of our inner selves, waiting for us to recognize it. This eternal world will come alive to us the moment we begin to reckon upon its reality. What do we mean by *reality*? That which has existence apart from any idea any mind may have of it, and which would exist if there were no mind anywhere to entertain a thought of it. That which is real has being in itself. It does not depend upon its observer for its validity.[14]

Recently, Joe and I were standing outside on a dark September night, observing one of the red moon eclipses. We could see it, but it was tiny compared to what it was in reality. When our neighbor brought out a telescopic camera lens, we were able to see much more. What we saw with our naked eye as just a little speck in the night sky was magnified with his telescopic lens.

When we attempt to see God and His purposes through the lens of our physical senses and limited perspective, He seems small and our problems large and out of control. But when we look at God through the telescope of His living Word, His eternal perspective, He lets us see just how big He is. We are then able to see our problems and losses within the scope of His eternal plan.

Chapter 22

Darkness

You cannot smile in the light of day
until you learn to sing in the dark of night.
—DEBBIE MAYER

Loss always brings change, and making adjustments is part of the process. The move to a new house made it even more obvious that my former life had ended, requiring more adjustments and accentuating the emptiness I already felt.

A few months before the girls died, after a fall in my living room, I needed an x-ray of my neck to see if I had a pinched nerve. The x-ray revealed something unrelated. My doctor discovered an abnormal growth of my thyroid called a goiter. Since I felt fine and my thyroid levels were normal, we decided to do nothing except keep an eye on it.

After Joe and I settled in our townhouse, my panic attacks subsided but at night I often found it hard to breathe and swallow, which added to the anxiety I already felt from moving. At night, I needed a light on, music playing, and often medication to sleep. Joe was so compassionate and understanding to put up with all of that while he tried to sleep.

After noticing the lump in my throat had grown, I went to the endocrinologist and found out the goiter had doubled in size and was growing inward, pressing on my windpipe and making it harder for me to swallow and breathe. It helped to know there was an actual physical reason for my anxiety. I eventually had my thyroid removed. I was thankful to hear the lump was not cancer, but not so happy about the way it hindered my voice for quite some time.

Before my surgery, I had been speaking at events. After surgery, I couldn't talk, which meant no public speaking for me for the next six months. After four months, my voice gradually returned, but I couldn't sing for more than a year. During the months my voice was healing, I received no speaking or singing invitations. Even though I was unable to speak, the lack of attention and invitations caused feelings of rejection to rise up.

In any loss, it is important to receive care and attention, and it was healing for both Joe and me to be cared for "as we were"—with unique needs. We realized how unintentionally we could begin to feel entitled, expecting that type of care to continue by placing unrealistic expectations on others. Our expectations could also set us up for disappointment, presenting an even greater sense of loneliness, which at times did just that.

Joe experienced this much earlier than I did, when he returned to his job. It was as if he wanted to say, "Don't you know who I am and what has happened to me?" But since I was in front of people more and given so much attention, I didn't encounter that kind of discouragement until the speaking and singing invitations stopped.

None of us have been created to be the center of attention; rather, we have been made to make Jesus Christ central in our life—in times of loss or blessing. We reflect the Son and shine like stars as we hold out His Word of life (Philippians 2:15). Unfortunately, circumstances can place any of us in the position to be tempted to think more of ourselves than we ought. If we give in to that temptation, it only leads to disappointment.

In retrospect, I see now that I needed to have that hidden time of quietness, away from the limelight and attention of people, to enter deeper into my pain. Although I wouldn't see it for a while, leaning into my loss, although quite painful, set me in a place to soak up God's blessings.

It took more than three years to get my singing voice back, and I eventually led worship again.

People looking at me from the outside perceived that things were going fine, but I felt disconnected with life. I did my best to remain involved with my commitments and relationships, reaching out to people in ways I was able. Realizing I could not depend on my feelings or circumstances because they were often sad and negative, I began to feel darkness deepening. C. S. Lewis described it well in *A Grief Observed*:

> No one ever told me that grief felt so like fear. I am not afraid, but the sensation is like being afraid. ... There is a sort of invisible blanket between the world and me. I find it hard to take in what anyone says. Or perhaps, hard to want to take it in. It is so uninteresting. Yet I want the others to be about me. I dread the moments when the house is empty.[15]

One night while missing the girls so much, I wrestled with believing whether God was good after all, feeling as if I would die from my pain. My mind echoed, *It's not fair! This is just too hard!* What I voiced was something consistent with those thoughts. I could see Joe wanted and needed to say something to me but he hesitated.

I prodded and then insisted, and in his gentle and diplomatic way, he said, "You're not the only one grieving, you know." Expounding, he said that I was acting as if I was the only one experiencing loss, but there were many more, including himself, Joey and Bree, Mom and Dad, the rest of the family, and the girls' friends.

I got the point.

At once, I became aware of the pain others might be feeling and wondered about their experiences with our loss. No one had shared them with me. Maybe I had made it hard for them to do so. I asked God to forgive my selfishness, and repented of giving in to self-pity, realizing that I would not move forward unless I remembered that others also struggled with grief.

It's one thing to receive instruction from others and even revelation from the Lord, but it usually takes time and practice for it to be established and worked into our everyday lives. This revelation was no different for me.

The process of grief does not happen in neat little steps you can orchestrate, but rather weaves in and out of a mourner's life. I discovered rather quickly that grief is more like a roller coaster, full of emotional ups and downs. It's not even one step forward and two steps back. It's often more like one step forward, three steps back, only to fall down before getting up again. However, I now realize setbacks are not always negative. We can progress in the midst of them—even because of them. Setbacks expose what's inside of us, teach us to care for others, and bring us to rely on the Lord.

More loss.

My sister Kathie had not been feeling well for quite some time. Two mornings after we celebrated what would have been Krista's twenty-sixth birthday with Kathie, her two daughters, and some friends, I learned Kathie had been admitted to a hospital.

When Joe and I reached the hospital floor she was on, the sign read *Oncology*. My heart sank.

We walked into her room, and with gut wrenching sobs, she blurted, "I'm dying!"

I asked, hardly able to believe it, "What did you say?"

After more heaving sobs, she said, "I have lung cancer and six months left to live."

I felt too stunned to speak.

My first thought was, *Lucky. She gets to go before me!* I embraced her, promising, "You will *not* have to walk through this alone."

I spent the next three nights with her in her hospital room, crying with her and encouraging her with Scriptures. The following three weeks I stayed with her in her home until I took turns with our siblings and her daughters for the next three months, so that she was never alone.

Two weeks before Kathie died, Buddy, our canine friend and comforter, died in his sleep at the foot of our bed. We lost his loyal companionship and sweet presence, the last tangible connection within our home associated with the girls. Both our hearts felt sad and yet thankful for the precious gift he had been to us.

When Kathie heard how he had died, she said, "I hope I can go as peacefully as him."

Her last days and hours were spent with family. We sang worship songs and spoke God's truths to her. She died in a peaceful way with her loved ones at her bedside, each one saying goodbye. Four months after her medical diagnosis, she went to heaven.

Kathie had been a single mother of three daughters. She was my sister and my friend. We spent a lot of time together, sharing our secrets and surviving many struggles. We laughed and cried together. We would talk for hours at a time. We did life together. She was one of my biggest cheerleaders. There will be no one to replace who she was to me in this world. Her passing became another hole in my heart and life.

Kathie's life continued on in perfect, eternal love and freedom in her new heavenly home with Jesus and my three daughters, while I remained here with her three daughters. I was glad she was free from pain, but the process of her dying was physically and emotionally draining, and my grief for the girls seemed to deepen.

Around the time we suffered the losses of Kathie and our dog, problems with Joe's job arose that completely drained our bank account. Dealing with the uncertainty of our future caused stress and tension in our relationship, exacerbating my already heavy heart.

Each time I began to feel some hope, it seemed another loss or disappointment came to sabotage me. My days grew darker. Instead of peace, I often felt fear. Instead of faith, doubt. Instead of dwelling on eternal life and the kingdom of God, I only saw barrenness.

Joe and I began to disengage a little in our relationship, although nothing was outwardly apparent. We distanced ourselves—and not just from each other but from everything. More so than Joe, I built walls of self-preservation from more pain.

Grief can accentuate every struggle you experience, exaggerating each negative thought and feeling. It seemed like barrenness was everywhere in my life. I began to doubt the goodness of God. A spiritual fog entered my mind, and, at times, I lost the sense of God's comforting presence. I had only what seemed like faint recollections of words and promises from an old Friend. All seemed dark.

Besides the lives God touched during the girls' funeral and in the months that followed, I had personally discipled and nurtured others over the years. But I saw or heard of a number of these individuals who slipped away from the Lord and returned to their old lifestyles. I surmised even the fruit of our kingdom ministry was dying too.

My life seemed like I was climbing a tree to look out above the forest, but each time I reached a higher branch, it would break and I'd plummet to the ground. Soon it felt as if the tree was barren with no branches left to even hang onto. I was stuck.

Longing for days when life was sweet and simple, I read in my Bible the words from Habakkuk 3:17–18. Then I remembered a song called "I Will Rejoice," which I had led in worship when Joey helped me on the worship team at church. The lyrics were based on that same Scripture, which says, "Though the fig tree does not bud and there are no grapes on the vines, though the olive crop fails and the fields produce no food, though there are no sheep in the pen and no cattle in the stalls, yet I will rejoice in the LORD, I will be joyful in God my Savior."

I groaned inwardly, realizing I had once sung that song with such enthusiasm. But now I wondered, *Do I even understand its words?* The words of the song expressed joy and faith in spite of seeing no fruit or blessings.

I tried to dwell on the truth of the Scripture and song—to rejoice in the Lord no matter what. But at the time, all I could think about was no buds, no grapes, no fruit.

Only barrenness.

Oh, how I wanted to experience the words of that song.

Around the same time, I read Charles Spurgeon's *Morning & Evening* devotional, which also used the word *barren*, but it cast a positive tone on my lack of fruit. I read that my barrenness was actually the means for God's fruit-creating power. A faint glimmer of light radiated into my darkness.

The devotional exhorted me, a barren woman, to sing for joy, offering me promises of God's compassion and help.

> "Sing, barren woman ... burst into song, shout for joy ..." says the LORD. ... "Do not be afraid; you will not be put to shame. Do not fear disgrace; you will not be humiliated. For your Maker is your husband—the LORD Almighty is his name—the Holy One of Israel is your Redeemer; he is called the God of all the earth. ... Though the mountains be shaken and the hills be removed, yet my unfailing love for you will not be shaken nor my covenant of peace be removed," says the LORD, who has compassion on you. ... "No weapon forged against you will prevail, and you will refute every tongue that accuses you. This is the heritage of the servants of the LORD, and this is their vindication from me," declares the LORD (ISAIAH 54:1, 4–5, 10, 17).

The words of this Scripture reverberated with what God had spoken to me years before in my dream about the demons of discouragement, despair, and depression that had threatened to kill me if I did not bow down to them. My victory would come from worshiping God. I knew if I chose to sing songs of praise in the night, with a thankful heart, I would somehow be able to smile when the morning came.

God encouraged me, meeting me in my barrenness, and spoke to me personally again and again. He reminded me of what He'd already said. I meditated on perfectly timed Scriptures and recalled this song in my dark night, with no other words to express myself.

Still, I felt empty.

While worshiping, I'd cry. While praying, I'd fall asleep. My faith felt weak. Although I believed in His goodness, it was so dark that all I could see at this point was barrenness, having lost my sense of identity and purpose.

Chapter 23

Remembering
the Signs

And whatever strange things may happen to you,
let nothing turn your mind from following the signs.
—*THE SILVER CHAIR* BY C. S. LEWIS

Even worship songs reminded me of my loss, bringing back memories of intimate times of worship I had shared with my girls, never to happen again on earth.

Growth brings change—especially letting go of the past. Emotional healing only results if we decide to act or think differently, allowing newness of life to form inside our hearts and minds. But if we're not ready to let go and accept uncontrollable changes that have altered our lives, or if we refuse to step up to a challenge, we remain stuck.

Stuck.

I was stuck in the place of barren and unfruitful. I was allowing those words to define me.

Whenever God is about to do a new thing, the devil will bring up an old thing. The old lie I fell for all over again was, *I'm a big loser!* However, this time an exclamation mark came at the end, threatening me to believe the rest of my life would be barren and unfruitful. Even God's Word seemed written in a foreign language. Reading a devotional book felt like deciphering secret code. One night as I read about the bride of Christ, it was only faintly discernable to my spirit. I felt as though I had spiritual amnesia—as if I had fallen into a strange trance.

Something was really wrong. My heart had grown cold. Not all the time, but a lot of the time. Enough to stifle my quality of life. I was gradually losing hope.

One day, while believing the lies that in my old age I would be barren, and that I was a loser with a capital "L," I desperately cried out to God. I asked Him to bring me out of this spiritual trance.

I could go through just about anything if I knew the truth of God's Word concerning whatever was happening. In this case, I needed to hear the voice of God's Word. I had been listening to the wrong voices. And I felt powerless.

Oh, please speak truth. Help me remember.

Before I went to bed, I picked up my Bible and turned to Isaiah 46. I intended to look up the verses about rejoicing in my barrenness, but God wanted to say something new. Instead I read verses 3–4: "'Listen … you whom I have upheld since your birth, and have carried since you were born. Even to your old age and gray hairs I am he, I am he who will sustain you. I have made you and I will carry you; I will sustain you and I will rescue you.'"

My merciful Savior reminded me once again of His unending love, saying, "I loved you then, I love you now and forever, and I will carry you until the end." Even in my old age!

Verse 5 continued, "'With whom will you compare me or count me equal? To whom will you liken me that we may be compared?'" I don't know why I was so surprised to see how specifically He responded and reminded me He is incomprehensible.

I-n-c-o-m-p-r-e-h-e-n-s-i-b-l-e. He has always been faithful. Why wouldn't He be now? During that time, I was listening to *The Silver Chair* on CD, part of The Chronicles of Narnia books by C. S. Lewis. While listening, God clarified what had happened in my own life.

In the allegorical story, Aslan (representing God) gave Jill (one of the characters whom he loved) four signs—promises and instructions she was supposed to remember and obey to guide her on her journey.

Aslan warned her that the air in his country (representing time in his presence) was clear, but as soon as she descended the mountain (the journey and struggle of life), her thinking could become muddled. He specifically told her, "Pay no attention to appearances. Remember the Signs and believe the Signs. Nothing else matters."[16] In Scripture, we are also told to walk by faith, not by sight, fixing our eyes on the unseen realities of heaven.

Jill soon forgot the Signs (God's truth) and focused only on her circumstances. She was misled by the false appearances of things around her. As I read, she too appeared to be in a trance and, because of this, was confronted with many dangers. I saw I had forgotten the many truths God had given me because I had focused on my losses instead of His truths—and I entered into a kind of trance.

Wanting all that God was showing me, I went back to read the rest of Isaiah 46. Verse 7 says the people made idols to pray to, yet their idols could not hear or save them from their distress. Reading that brought Psalm 135:16–18 to mind, which had made an impression on me years earlier, concerning idols: "They have mouths, but cannot speak, eyes, but cannot see. They have ears, but cannot hear, nor is there breath in their mouths. Those who make them will be like them, and so will all who trust in them."

Wow. I realized that while focusing on my losses, I had actually made idols of them. My losses had gradually become what I worshiped, and now they were sucking the breath (life) right out of me. I had not meant to make them idols, but my losses outweighed everything. I had become stuck in my grief.

We are created to worship, and whatever has our greatest attention or focus is what we worship. According to God's Word, we will be like whatever we worship.

This revelation woke me from my trance.

I thought my focus had become divided between my losses and my God, but I discovered that's not possible because we cannot serve two masters. Jesus spoke of this principle in the parable of the two masters in the Gospels of Matthew and Luke. Our worship to God cannot be divided. We will love one and hate the other or be devoted to one and despise the other. *Am I in danger of hating my Savior? My Best Friend? My heavenly Bridegroom?*

The thought made me ill. But anything can become an idol if it distracts us from the One who loves us most.

The fact that I had made an idol of my losses and was believing lies about God sobered me. I remembered a pencil drawing I found that Krista sketched on the back of the church bulletin while listening to Pastor Mike preach on repentance. The message communicated by the image she sketched was so clear in my mind. Repentance is turning away from the sin and turning to God. It's an attitude of openness to God that allows us to be changed as we align our thoughts with His truth.

Turn to Repent – Krista's pencil sketch

I repented for focusing more on my losses than on God, and for believing lies about Him. I hardly needed help from Satan to think negative thoughts about myself, but he had also spoken negative thoughts and accusations to me about God, causing me to question His character.

Satan also used this tactic on Eve. First, he told her she wouldn't die if she ate the fruit, which directly contradicted what God had told her. Then he told her God knew her eyes would be opened when she ate the fruit and then she'd be like Him, which led her to believe God didn't have her best in mind. Eve misjudged God's heart and character, which led her to wrong actions.

Satan continually accuses God in our minds because if we think wrongly about God, we will think wrongly about ourselves and our situations, influencing everything we do.

At this point I realized my vulnerability had opened a door that strengthened a network of lies. The root lie I believed made me vulnerable to the enemy. Typically, a repeated phrase passes through the mind, then comes out of the mouth.

I had two lies—two phrases: *If God loved me so much, why all this pain?* and *It's not fair!* I said these statements when I was alone. They allowed the devil to infiltrate my thoughts and accuse God of being unkind and unjust. The lies accused God's character and essentially said that what Jesus did on the cross was not enough for me. By identifying these lies, I could reclaim the ground I'd given the enemy.

Joe pointed out that my idea of fairness was based on human standards. But God is beyond fair—He is merciful. He displays kindness and mercy daily in what He's created and what He's creating in me.

As I continued reading Isaiah 46, I read, "Remember the former things, those of long ago; I am God, and there is no other; I am God, and there is none like me. I make known the end from the beginning, from ancient times, what is still to come. I say, My purpose will stand, and I will do all that I please" (Isaiah 46:9–10). His purposes will stand. I had to remember the signs God gave me and take back the ground I had given the enemy.

It amazes me that even when I focused on my losses, God

demonstrated mercy toward me and drew my attention back to Him. That's what His Word does in such a personal way. Psalm 139:3 says He is familiar with all our ways. God didn't condemn or shame me. Instead, He reminded me that He is God and He loves me and is always near, even when I think or feel the opposite is true.

> Where can I go from your Spirit? Where can I flee from your presence? If I go up to the heavens, you are there; if I make my bed in the depths, you are there. If I rise on the wings of the dawn, if I settle on the far side of the sea, even there your hand will guide me, your right hand will hold me fast. If I say, "Surely the darkness will hide me and the light become night around me, even the darkness will not be dark to you; the night will shine like the day, for darkness is as light to you." (Psalm 139:7–12)

Although I had repented and began to resist dwelling on my losses, I still did not see much fruit in my life or in the lives of those I had invested my time and energy in. I was still tempted to be sad even while endeavoring to believe the Word of God.

I read something that spoke about the "day of in between." Once a year, our emphasis is on Good Friday and Easter Sunday. But what about the day in between? What about Silent Saturday?

We know that from heaven's perspective, it was not silent at all. Jesus was engaged in accomplishing the Father's will, leading to Resurrection Sunday. But to His disciples, it was a time of silent inactivity, lost dreams, and shattered faith. To them, and to all of us who experience a "day of in between," it represents death, lost hope, inactivity, and no signs of life. The end of a good thing. No fruit.

This time can also be described as a waiting time—we are waiting to see if we will ever see fruit or come alive again. And even if we believe we will, we still have to wait for it. It's so hard to wait when you see no signs of life. In reality, the paradox is that God was doing His greatest work of all time during that apparent "dead" time.

I was reminded once again of the truth from John 12:24: "Unless a kernel of wheat falls to the ground and dies, it remains only a single seed. But if it dies, it produces many seeds." The tomb and these kernels of wheat were symbolic of my life—a lot of dying. Dying to my own thoughts, feelings, preconceived ideas, and expectations of life and how I thought it should be. Dying to my old life.

And a lot of waiting. Waiting to feel better. Waiting for the fulfillment of promises I believed God had given me through His Word. And a lot of changing, although I didn't see it at the time.

During this season, I was especially encouraged by Galatians 6:9: "Let us not become weary in doing good, for at the proper time we will reap a harvest if we do not give up."

I understood the principle of sowing and reaping because I loved working in my flower garden. If I plant zinnia seeds, I reap zinnia flowers. The same is true in our thought life. If I plant seeds of faith, I reap spiritual fruit. But if I plant seeds of negativity, I reap negativity.

According to Isaiah 55:10–12, if I sow His Word, I will reap truth: "As the rain and the snow come down from heaven, and do not return to it without watering the earth and making it bud and flourish, so that it yields seed for the sower and bread for the eater, so is my word that goes out from my mouth: It will not return to me empty, but will accomplish what I desire and achieve the purpose for which I sent it."

I knew if I stayed in the light of God's Word, His truth would grow inside me.

After moving to our new house, God had given me the word *metamorphosis* to explain the excruciating pain I had been experiencing. When words pop into my head, even if I know what they basically mean, I often look up their definition to learn something from them about my situation.

The dictionary used the word *transform* in the description of *metamorphosis*, which we know to be a change, either outwardly or inwardly and by supernatural or natural means. These ideas encouraged me with a promise of hope that things would not always be as they were. I called this season my "metamorphosis of grief."

A friend knew I was interested in butterflies and gave me two caterpillars with some milkweed. I conducted my own little experiment with the caterpillars, documenting each phase they went through with photos and videos. I watched as each of them ate the milkweed, climbed a twig I had placed in the jar, and then formed a chrysalis.

I waited.

Inside the dark chrysalis a transformation was occurring, but I couldn't see it. If I cut open the cocoon to see the growth, I would kill it. The caterpillar's change required struggle. But the struggle was inside its cocoon. There's no other way.

The same is true for seeds planted in soil. They have to stay buried to sprout. Underground—in the tomb, so to speak—is where they have to stay if they are going to grow and blossom into new life.

The same is true with our spiritual life. If I wanted to see fruit in my life, I would have to wait. I would have to trust the Gardener of my life for my transformation. This in-between time, with no apparent signs of change from the outside, was critical to the new life being formed within me. I had to patiently wait.

I discovered that what I did during this waiting time inside my "cocoon," when no one else could see me, was very important, because that's when my motives were purified.

In the Bible, waiting does not mean passive inactivity. It means taking action by looking to God with expectancy. It is trusting. Waiting considers God's love, His character, and His promises. I could not go by my feelings or embrace each random thought that entered my mind. I chose to take my thoughts captive, trusting that God was absolutely for me, not against me, not even indifferent to me.

If I wanted to reap good fruit, I would have to sow good thoughts. Thoughts of truth, not lies. Thoughts of God's goodness, not my barrenness. To go forward I needed to remember the signs of God's promises and instructions He had given me throughout my journey, recalling my history with Him.

Chapter 24

Signs of Hope

We move into the future not with a map, a plan, or a clear structure,
but with the whisper of a story that reminds us we will
again see the goodness of God in the land of the living.
—THE HEALING PATH BY DAN ALLENDER

Going forward does not mean we will progress without pain. Usually we go forward, remembering the signs and God's promises and instructions, while we still hurt, to lay hold of our healing. Remembering the signs not only means being intentional about our thought life, but also putting actions to our intentions.

One way I did this was by repenting of dwelling on my losses and speaking negative words. The Greek word for *repentance* is *metanoia*, which means "a change of mind,"[17] or to think differently, so I had to replace the old with the new. I had to think and believe in God's goodness.

To believe in God's goodness, I determined to quit dwelling on my losses, and stop the negative self-talk. Pastor and author Rick Warren says, "Long before psychology came around, God said your thoughts determine your feelings, and your feelings determine your actions. If you want to change your life, you have to control the way you think."[18] I have come to see that it's easy to get caught in my own story—thinking that I was the only one on the planet and believing everything I thought or felt was true.

When training my muscles, the more curls I do with weights,

the firmer my biceps and triceps become. The same is true for my thoughts. The more energy and effort I give to a thought, the stronger it becomes until it births an action. But overcoming the thought life is a process. First I needed to think differently, then speak differently, and finally—act differently.

I realized I didn't have to go through life as a victim of my feelings and circumstances. That's not freedom. That's why we are told in Scripture to take our thoughts captive to Christ.

Easier said than done.

On too many occasions, my words spoke contrary to God's Word, which only led me back into despair, building a wall in my relationship with God and sometimes with others. I needed and wanted to think and speak right.

In Lamentations 3:19–20, the writer remembered his affliction and how his soul was downcast within him. But in verses 21–24 he called to mind God's great compassion and faithfulness in an effort to regain his hope. Afterward, he said to himself, "The Lord is good to those who hope in him" (v. 24). I spent too much time listening to myself. I should have been calling to mind and listening to God. Then I would speak God's truth within me: *He is good to me.*

In Psalm 42:5, the writer asked himself, "Why are you downcast, O my soul?" Then he instructed his soul, "Put your hope in God, for I will yet praise him, my Savior and my God." This showed me how to deal with conflicting thoughts. To change a thought, I simply needed to stop and replace it with another. The same is true with our words.

The *Treasury of David* commentary says, "As though he were two men, the psalmist talks to himself. His faith reasons with his fears, and his hope argues with his sorrows."[19] This helped me.

Verse 7 says "deep calls to deep." God answers the depth of our weakness with the depth of His strength. As a lot of us know, life can be going great and suddenly we are pulled under by waves of sorrow and loss. But since we were created to experience intimacy with God, His mercy draws us back the moment we call out to Him.

From my pain, loss, loneliness, and fear, I looked to God, who knows the end from the beginning within the mystery of His sovereignty and eternal love. This was the same God whose ears heard my cries and reached down into the deep waters of my dark night to draw me out. As I called out to God from the depths of my soul, exercising my faith, God began to meet me there.

The choice was mine.

We were not created to be robots, programmed to automatically respond to God's commands and truths. He created us with the freedom to live life our own way or to call out to Him in dependence. He never forces us to trust Him. I could continue in my current mode of spiritual sickness disguised as coping, or I could take every thought captive to Christ and be healed and set free.

God provided all the armor and weapons I needed to live a life of victory, but if I ignored them, I would live a defeated life. I asked God for help and soon came up with a battle plan. I called it "The Triple A Plan." I needed to:

1. *Agree* with God's Word
2. *Articulate* God's Word
3. *Act* on God's Word

It was hard at first, because for so long, I was in the habit of freely verbalizing each negative thought and feeling. It's not that I always spoke these things out loud, but I said them to myself. I have learned that what I speak to myself matters most, because that is what I act on. And our actions eventually affect others.

I saw that when I spoke negative thoughts aloud, not only was I speaking lies and damaging words to myself, but also to Joe and others, affecting the atmosphere around me. Joe was patient, as usual, but I literally spoke gloom into our home and relationship.

As I became more aware of what I was doing, I counteracted the negativity by speaking God's truth rather than fear into my home and our relationship. This release of faith made a difference. I wrote Scripture verses on index cards and placed them in noticeable locations throughout our house. I began memorizing Scripture again and listening to Bible teachings. I gradually began to take command over my fears. I looked to God in faith and remembered His words of life to me. I argued with my sorrow by hoping in God's goodness.

I practiced taking my thoughts captive to Christ and making them obedient to Him, which demolished the devil's arguments and my own reasoning that was usually against the knowledge of God. What I said outwardly began to conform to God's truth within me. As I did this with greater intention, I began to see signs of hope in my life, and my relationship with Joe thrived once again.

Psalm 27:12–14 spoke directly to me and my circumstances: "Do not turn me over to the desire of my foes, for false witnesses rise up against me, spouting malicious accusations. I remain confident of this: I will see the goodness of the LORD in the land of the living. Wait for the LORD; be strong and take heart and wait for the LORD."

My enemies were not men in armor pursuing me; they were the words and lies of my old thinking patterns and the enemy, who wanted to destroy me and my relationship with God and others. God graciously gave me this Scripture, and I repeated it daily as a verbal weapon: "I remain confidant of this: I will see the goodness of the LORD in the land of the living. Wait for the LORD; be strong and take heart and wait for the LORD" (PSALM 27:13–14).

Shortly after God gave me this Scripture, Pastor Mike asked me to sing the song "You Are Good" during both services at church every Sunday in the month of December. The lyrics speak of God's overwhelming goodness. I thought, *The same song every Sunday? Both services? How strange.* But the sermon series was "The Goodness of God," and God seemed serious in wanting me (along with others) to get it.

Each Sunday service when I sang the song, I struggled to believe the words. *This really is true, isn't it?* As I thought about the lessons I had recently learned about the seed, the chrysalis, the tomb, and not growing weary, I confronted my feelings of doubt with God's truth and brought to mind the signs God had given me.

Oswald Chambers once said, "God does not give us overcoming life: He gives us life as we overcome."[20] I believe this refers to the struggle we encounter that is necessary to be transformed. Waiting, pressing, struggling. These all describe the practice of faith. Living with hope. We move forward with faith and hope, not without fear but in the midst of it. *Oxford Living Dictionary's* definition of *courage* is "strength in the face of pain or grief."[21] And that is what hope enables us to do.

One morning during this season of waiting and remembering, I was reading my Bible. A verse in John 11 caught my attention. Lazarus had died, and when Jesus came to the tomb, He became emotionally moved. He asked some men to take away the stone, and Martha reminded Him that Lazarus had been dead for four days and there would be a terrible stench. Her brother was dead and there were no signs of hope, just stinky decay.

But God is never afraid of the stench that death produces in our lives because He is life. Jesus reproved her in verse 40: "Did I not tell you that if you believe, you will see the glory of God?" The moment I read these words, it was as if God whispered a secret to me from His very heart.

Jesus reminded Martha of their earlier conversation when He told her that He was the resurrection and the life and that anyone who believed in Him would live, even though they died. He was talking about more than restoring physical life to Lazarus when He said she would see the glory of God. He was saying He would display His power and goodness no matter how bleak the situation was. He would demonstrate that *He* was the resurrection and the life. He was disappointed she did not believe Him. He had just given her *the* biggest sign of hope ever given to anyone.

As I read what exchanged between them, I felt the Lord stirring up hope in me to believe the instructions and promises He had given to me—to believe in His goodness and power and every word of His, because He can give life to the lifeless. His words are spirit and life because He is the living Word. If I believe in Him and what He promises me, I will see His glory—no matter what the circumstances may be.

A friend had invited me to a conference at a church near my house. During the ministry time, I went forward for prayer. The only words I shared with the people who were ready to pray for me was that I was coming out of a dark night. As they prayed, they asked God to "help me believe so I could see His glory." Their words in prayer filled me with great expectation and hope, knowing it was God wanting me to experience His glory, which is life.

The very next morning I shared my testimony while visiting another church. I spoke about the new things God was doing in my heart about believing. On the wall directly in front of me was a banner that read, *Expect His Glory!* I knew this was God's declaration to me, inviting me to believe it.

Yes, expect His glory!

At that moment, I felt the tug of the Holy Spirit inviting me to let go of my fears and confidently hope in Him. Scripture tells us that hope that is seen is no hope at all. Who hopes for what they already have? But if we hope for what we do not already have, we wait for it patiently (Romans 8:24–25). This was not just a nugget of truth, it was a mountain!

During that season, I had been finding it difficult to engage in conversations and activities involving other families. Nevertheless, I visited a good friend in another state. Her whole family was around her a lot of the time, and her adult children were the same ages my girls would have been. I was happy for her but felt taunted by all the life she enjoyed. Somehow it felt easier to just exist than to enter into another family's life. I struggled to not project into my current circumstances what I saw as my barren future.

Enjoying the moment I was in was difficult. The intense grief that had engulfed me for so long began to diminish, but then suddenly it would overwhelm me again. Focusing on my sorrow had become such a familiar, secure place that it was hard to remain in a place of letting go of it. I so wanted to enjoy and engage in an entire moment without grief.

God knew this, of course, and orchestrated an experience for me, my moment of glory. I went to a worship service and became enraptured by a song that surrounded me with God's presence. Totally oblivious to everyone around me, I was able to focus on those moments I had with the Lord as if it was just God and me. I had experienced other intimate times with the Lord, but there was something special about those glorious moments. I just stood there weeping as I heard God's gentle whispers call forth a heart response from me to embrace, engage, and enjoy the moment I was in. The love I felt invited me to embrace life.

I'd once heard someone say that memories are gifts but are only meant for visits, not to take up residency in us. When I dwell on the past, longing to go back, there is nothing I can do but be sad. When I worry about the future with its uncertainty and unpredictability, I get anxious. Either option robs me of the here and now, leaving me hopeless and preventing me from the very life Jesus longs to give me.

On my plane flight home, I picked up a magazine in the seat pocket in front of me. On the cover was Serena Williams tossing a tennis ball. I read about what makes athletes winners. It described a person's sweet spot, the place in which his or her energy flows. Tony Hawk, one of the best skateboarders in the world, said that even when things don't go right, he tries to enjoy the ride and have fun.

Wow, he's talking about my life. I definitely need to learn to enjoy the ride more.

God is always speaking to us, and He often uses everyday things. Even airplane magazines. He wanted me to enjoy the present moments throughout my life, whether with Him or with others. It's a gift. That's why it's called the present. It's the only time we have. The past is gone; the future is not yet.

Whether focusing on my fears, lies about my losses, or the uncertainty of my future, I was being robbed of the present moment, causing me to feel detached from people and life. But when I focused on God's goodness, I experienced hope and was able to enjoy the moment. That's because it is a living hope (1 Peter 1:3–9). This living hope is not something we merely wish for, but it is solid and sure, an anchor for the soul. This living hope empowers us to live now, so that dying will be gain.

This living hope compelled me to live fully in the present, all the while investing in and preparing myself for eternity, which will be the total fulfillment of my hope. I look forward to my future glory, an inheritance in heaven that will never perish, spoil, or fade. These verses propelled me forward with joy and hopeful expectation: "Though you have not seen him, you love him; and even though you do not see him now, you believe in him and are filled with an inexpressible and glorious joy, for you are receiving the end result of your faith, the salvation of your souls" (1 Peter 1:8–9).

After Jessica died, her art teacher gave me a chalk drawing Jess had made in her seventh-grade art class. As I looked at the picture, with the sun rising from the water over the horizon, I felt a warm and inviting energy radiating peace and healing into me. I thought of the promise in Malachi 4:2: "But for you who fear My name, the sun of righteousness will rise with healing in its wings" (NASB). I knew that as I feared God, looking to the Son of Righteousness, my healing and hope would continue to rise with songs of praise and take wings. I am thankful Jess made this beautiful picture titled "Creating a Brighter Tomorrow."

Creating a Brighter Tomorrow – Jessica's chalk drawing

Chapter 25

Will the Real Debbie Please Stand Up?

We are intimately loved long before our parents,
teachers, spouses, children and friends loved or wounded us.
That's the truth of our lives. That's the truth spoken
by the voice that says, "You are my Beloved."
—LIFE OF THE BELOVED BY HENRI NOUWEN

Early on in my grief, I received a letter from a woman I didn't know who had lost a child. She said the loss was like suddenly having an amputation without anesthesia, which gave me permission to feel my pain at the time. Later in my grief, I read what Jerry Sittser described as phantom pains in his book *A Grace Disguised*. He wrote, "Amputees often feel phantom pains. The limb they lost still announces its presence through pain."[22] Phantom pains of my former identity, which was primarily *mother*, lingered for a long time, reminding me of what I had lost. I still thought of myself as a mother to Joey, Krista, Nikki, and Jessica, but the only person on this earth who could define me as such no longer needed my care, because, as the saying goes, "Your son is your son till he marries a wife. Your daughter's your daughter for the rest of your life."

Joey's life was now joined with Bree's, so my relationship with him changed as suddenly as the loss of my girls. I loved my daughter-in-law very much, grateful to have her and delighted in who she was to Joe and me and especially to Joey. However, a mother relates to her daughter-in-law differently than she does with her own daughter. Suddenly, my new role with a married son and daughter-in-law felt vague and unclear to me, leaving me insecure as the mother I'd been so accustomed to being.

This was unmapped territory. I also needed to sort out my new role in my extended family. So many conversations and so much of how I had related to others was closely connected to being a mother to Joey, Krista, Nikki, and Jessica. Before the girls died, I had been involved in their schools and in my community. Now I lived in a new neighborhood with a new church and new house. Nothing was familiar.

I sang at a church function after it had been a long time since I'd done so. Several people came up to me afterward and said, "I didn't know you sang!" Taken aback, I realized that people no longer identified me as a singer. Then, after not speaking for a time, I was invited to speak somewhere. In reality, though, I no longer functioned as "Debbie the speaker." What did seem to identify me was "Debbie, the mother who lost her three daughters."

I felt branded like Scarboy, a character marked by his past from a children's allegory *Tales of the Kingdom* by David and Karen Mains. Although I resisted the temptation to think of myself as a loser, I felt insecure in my shaky, undefined identity, and uncertain about myself, my role in life, and my message.

What does my brighter tomorrow look like? Who am I anyway?

God used my brother-in-law to speak a word of life to me. He told me that God called me His bride long before my girls were even born, and that the story of my girls was not what defined me. I had not shared my struggle about my loss of identity with him, which made me take note. Recognizing God's intervention, his inspired words hit home.

I began to remember my true identity. What defined me most wasn't being a wife, mother, host for family get-togethers, singer, or volunteer leader in church and community. In fact, my worth and identity wasn't in any of these roles. But now that a lot of the external things I thought identified me had been stripped from me, or shaken, I could see my identity was not attached to anything outward.

I am not defined by what I do or don't do. I am defined by God. I am whomever He calls me, and all that matters is what He says and knows about me. He wonderfully calls me His bride, His beloved. There is nothing I can do to make Him love me more, and nothing I can do—or ever did—that can make Him love me less. I accepted the truth that if no one else knew who I was, God did. I was ready to receive my identity as the one God said I was.

Reading the words from Henri Nouwen's *Life of the Beloved*, my heart was reminded to once again receive the endearing words God had spoken early on in my relationship with Him about my real identity.

Listening to that voice with great inner attentiveness, I hear at my center the words that say: "I have called you by name, from the very beginning. You are mine and I am yours. You are my Beloved, on you my favor rests. I have molded you in the depths of the earth and knitted you together in your mother's womb. I have carved you in the palms of my hands and hidden you in the shadow of my embrace. I look at you with infinite tenderness and care for you with a care more intimate than that of a mother for her child. I have counted every hair on your head and guided you at every step. Wherever you go, I go with you, and wherever you rest, I keep watch. I will give you food that will satisfy all your hunger and drink that will quench all your thirst. I will not hide my face from you. You know me as your own and I know you as my own. You belong to me. I am your father, your mother, your brother, your sister, your lover, and your spouse ... yes, even your child ... wherever you are I will be. Nothing will ever separate us. We are one." ... Every time you listen with great attentiveness

199

to the voice that calls you the Beloved, you will discover within yourself a desire to hear that voice longer and more deeply. It is like discovering a well in the desert. Once you have touched wet ground, you want to dig deeper.[23]

When interviewed for a *Los Angeles Times* article, Nouwen stated simply, "Spiritual identity means we are not what we do or what people say about us. We are the beloved."[24]

While at a women's function at church, I observed God raise up ordinary women who, up to that point, had been in the background. While contemplating this in my bed that night, I saw a vision. It was like a movie before me, as real as the room I was in.

I saw a beautiful bride lying on the floor, sleeping on her side. She slowly opened her eyes and elegantly rose up enough to rest on her elbow. Looking around with delight, she lifted herself to her knees. She did not wipe her eyes as one typically does when waking up, nor did she need to adjust her dress in any way. She looked poised, radiant, and alert. Most of all, she was *ready*.

At that moment, a hand came into view. I knew this was the Bridegroom's hand, and He gently helped her rise to her feet. She stood with ease and composed confidence. Humility and dignity adorned her. I understood in my spirit that God was not upset with her for sleeping because He had been preparing her, and now she was ready.

A Scripture came to my mind: "Arise, my darling, my beautiful one, come with me" (Song of Solomon 2:10). I discerned God was showing me that He was awakening His bride, His church, made up of ordinary people whose hearts are surrendered to Him. My vision was, I realized, also about me. The Lord had awakened me from my slumber of grief.

Once again, God reminded me that I am His bride. He reached for me, inviting me to respond to His invitation of love, and I took His hand. I was ready, with the confidence He'd given me, to enjoy His fellowship and partnership in ministry.

The enemy wants to prevent us from moving forward and will do anything to keep us in the past, which puts up a wall between us and God, stripping us of our true identity. The devil can't stand the fact that we are created in the image of God for His glory. Our enemy's goal is to keep us from experiencing intimacy with God. If he can keep us from knowing our true identity as God's beloved, then he has struck God's heart dead-on.

Intimacy with God looks like this: He is my Father—I am His child. He is my Bridegroom—I am His bride. He is the head of the church—I am a uniquely gifted member of His body. The Bible tells us in 1 John 4:8 that "God is love." That's the essence of His character.

God didn't just say, "I love you." He showed it. The most familiar Bible verse that best explains God's active love is John 3:16: "For God so loved the world that he gave his one and only Son, that whoever believes in him shall not perish but have eternal life." This speaks of God the Father's loving promise for the bride He purchased for His Son. The reason He gave so much makes what He gave so important. Love moved Him to give His Son for our sakes. As for the Son, we are the joy set before Him that moved Him to endure the cross.

God gave us the capacity, over all creation, to reflect His love as His image-bearers. He created us as unique individuals, and because of that our diverse relationships with Him, and personal expressions of love, will all be unique. The ways in which we experience Him will flow from who we are to Him and our personal stories with Him.

As I remembered and embraced the signs God had given me on my faith journey, I began to hope in my future again, which stirred up longing to be in His presence. As I spent more and more time alone with Him, I felt His love and affirmation once again. My hope, anchored in heaven, gave me eternal perspective, even though I was still unsure of what my future in this life held. I once again found it hard to suppress God's love and keep it to myself as in the early days with Him. I returned to my first love (Revelation 2:4).

I soon embraced the significant roles and relationships in my life with whom I could express this love. Besides being a wife and mother to my married son, I was also a daughter, sister, aunt, niece, cousin, friend, mentor, neighbor, and grandmother. "Mimi Debbie" to be exact, as Vivien, Joey and Bree's little girl, named me. I'm ever so grateful for this gift of life from God. My precious granddaughter added new joy to our family and my heart.

Because we are made in the image of God, whose essence is to lovingly give, we actually cease to live when we cease to love. After surviving a life-threatening illness, Norman Cousins said, "Death is not the greatest loss in life. The greatest loss is what dies inside us while we live."[25]

I realized a huge part of my identity as the bride of Christ was to be expressed in the relationships I had at the present time. Joe was the closest person to me. The more I became aware of being Christ's bride, I could then live more fully as Joe's bride.

While focusing on my losses, I had taken my role as Joe's wife for granted; worse, I had taken Joe for granted. He had always been so faithful and consistent, never demanding anything from me; he was always there for me. My appreciation for him grew as I remembered what a loving reflection of the Lord he was to me. God gave me some of Jesus when He gave me Joe.

My sister Sandy gave me a Christmas gift with the message, "Love isn't love till you give it away." That phrase summed up a lot of what I was learning about my identity and God's love for me. This song came from that experience. It's called "Give It Away":

> I thank my God for sending His Son for me.
> I thank my God for laying down all for me.
> When He gave His life for me, He forgave and set me free.
> Now I see how much He really loves me.
> Love isn't love till you give it away.
> I walk hand in hand with the King of Love today.
> He's so true. He's so kind. He always takes the time
> To find a way to love me in my every day.
> I thank my God for giving you to me.
> I thank my God, He knows just what I need.

When He gave you to me, He gave His gift of love so free.
Now I see how much He really loves me.
When you tell me that you love me, I hear the voice of God.
When you overlook my weakness, I see His heart of love.
When you see the dreams within me and help reach my goals,
I've tasted heaven's beauty, I'm healed and made whole!
Love is patient, love is kind, it does not envy anytime;
Love's not proud, nor is it rude, love hates evil and loves the truth.
Love protects, forgets the wrong, seeks not its own, love is strong.

Love. Serve. Build. I heard these three words within me as clear as ever, describing how I was to specifically express God's love right where I am, with the people and situations now present in my life.

Love: "Jesus replied: 'Love the Lord your God with all your heart and with all your soul and with all your mind. This is the first and greatest commandment. And the second is like it: Love your neighbor as yourself'" (Matthew 22:37–39).

God brought me back to the basics of what He showed me long ago: Love Him with everything in me, then love others. Only this time I saw something else—love and accept myself with God-centered, not self-absorbed, love. He reminded me to be intentional about what I thought and verbalized—to say and do everything in a spirit of love.

Serve: "You, my brothers and sisters, were called to be free. But do not use your freedom to indulge the flesh; rather, serve one another humbly in love. For the entire law is fulfilled in keeping this one command: 'Love your neighbor as yourself'" (Galatians 5:13–14).

My freedom was never meant to serve me and my personal happiness. Freedom is the desire, ability, and power to consider and work for the happiness of others as much myself. I felt compelled to find ways I could serve others to demonstrate God's love.

Build: "So Christ himself gave the apostles, the prophets, the evangelists, the pastors and teachers, to equip his people for works of service, so that the body of Christ may be built up until we all reach unity in the faith and in the knowledge of the Son of God and become mature, attaining to the whole measure of the fullness of Christ" (Ephesians 4:11–13).

A long time ago, God had stirred up the desire in me to be part of the larger body of Christ, and He now renewed that passion. I saw myself within His "one body" just as every believer is called to build the church at large in the unique way he or she can. I realized God deposited something of Himself in each of His own, including me— and I had a purpose to fulfill.

I took Jesus' hand and stepped out of self-preservation, revived. He gave me desire to be part of something much bigger than my personal story. My story of loss and faith is part of God's eternal story.

With each kind word and each act of compassion, I not only store up treasures in heaven, but also fulfill my part in the kingdom of heaven right now. What I did ten years ago may not be the same expression of God's love I offer now, or what I may offer ten years from now. Luke 16:10 reminds me that he who is faithful in little will be faithful in much. I asked myself, *Is it enough to simply be Debbie, beloved of God—period?* Not Debbie the singer or Debbie the speaker or Debbie the … whatever role that may still come. Is it all right to be Debbie who lives a quiet life loving God and others, whom nobody necessarily knows but is known by God as Debbie beloved of God?

As I invest in relationships with other broken people, my empathy and compassion comes from my own pain and loss. I can *love*, *serve*, and *build* the kingdom in ways unique to me because, I can now say, at least to a small degree, that I am broken bread and poured-out wine.

In a pamphlet on grief called "How Can I Live with My Loss?" Tim Jackson says, "Those who look at others through tears of grief have a perspective the dry-eyed cannot see, and they are uniquely qualified to minister to others in pain."[26]

What I do may change, but nothing can change who I am in Christ. I am Debbie, bride of Christ, beloved of God.

Part Six

PRESSING ON

Chapter 26

Embracing Life

To love abundantly is to live abundantly,
and to love forever is to live forever.
—HENRY DRUMMOND

Now that God had awakened me from my trance, reminding me of my identity as His bride, I began to live again. As my former pastor would say, "It feels good to feel good." Embracing life again meant doing the ordinary daily tasks of life without the feeling of dread. It meant being present and engaging with people, and enjoying movies, concerts, food, and other forms of entertainment.

When we enjoy God's gifts, we draw closer to Him because He's a good Father who loves to give good gifts to His children. He wants us to enjoy life. But if we allow His gifts to become the central focus of our lives as a source of comfort, they can usurp first place. We set ourselves up to be let down by looking to the gifts instead of the Giver. Always wanting more. With this mentality, nothing ever satisfies. I call this living a mediocre life—settling for less than the best. Good things, activities, and experiences are good, but God is better.

A. W. Tozer describes mediocre as "having a great peak before you and the dark valley below, and being stuck part way up the peak."[27]

It's so easy to land in this place if we take our gaze off of Jesus. It's really no different for someone who's grieving than for anyone on their journey on the path of life. If we seek things and experiences to satisfy us, life will turn into a series of highs and lows, producing no passion or joy for the things of God. Mark 8:36 says, "What good is it for someone to gain the whole world, yet forfeit their soul?"

C. S. Lewis explained mediocrity so well in *The Weight of Glory*:

The books or the music in which we thought the beauty was located will betray us if we trust to them; it was not in them, and what came through them was longing. These things—the beauty, the memory of our own past—are good images of what we really desire—but if they are mistaken for the thing itself, they turn into dumb idols breaking the hearts of their worshipers. For they are not in the thing itself, they are only the scent of a flower we have not found, the echo of a tune we have not heard, news from a country we have never yet visited.[28]

Since my real citizenship is in heaven, I decided to prioritize storing up things that will last forever. "For where your treasure is, there your heart will be also" (Matthew 6:21).

In *The Lord of the Rings*, Frodo reached Rivendell on his journey to destroy the ring. Rivendell was a resting place where he received healing, refreshment, and renewal, but it was not his journey's end. In the book *Finding God in The Lord of the Rings,* I read: "To mistake the inn for the journey's end is to fail altogether. It's to play into the enemy's hand."[29] There's a great temptation to remain in the comfort that things and experiences can bring.

Every year, I go on a little outdoor getaway with a dear friend. While hiking at a favorite spot, we start at the bottom of a steep, rocky trail with quite a bit of energy, but as we move toward the top, we take frequent rest stops. When we do, we enjoy the beautiful view, refresh ourselves with water, and snap a few pictures. But if we want to make it to the top, which is our goal, we must start moving again—soon. In life, it's important to enjoy the beauty and refreshment along the way, but if we get distracted from our goal and settle for lesser things, we will miss out on the bigger view at the top.

I have learned there are no substitutes for the abundant life God offers. The lesser things we settle for will look different to each of us, but will end up replacing the real thing and lead us in the opposite direction of God. If anything becomes more important to us than God and loving others, we will always want more and never be satisfied.

God spoke to my heart about this: *Why just survive when you can thrive? Why just exist when you can flourish? Why just settle when you can lay a hold of all I have for you?*

As I thought about these questions, I kept seeing the word LIFE in an acrostic with this message:

> L—Living
> I—Intentionally
> F—Free for
> E—Eternity

Tragedy has a way of sucking us into ourselves and our own interests, but God's love is a gift and the only antidote that can conquer our emptiness and self-interest. He drew me out of my self-focus to embrace real life. Real life is expressed and experienced in loving God and others. Galatians 5:6b says, "The only thing that counts is faith expressing itself through love." The only way to live intentionally free for eternity is to know and remain in this love.

Responding to God's love is the only thing that has brought fulfillment and lasting healing in my life. In John 15:9–13, Jesus tells me I can be filled with joy and fully alive by knowing I am valued and loved by God, and by loving others as I am loved:

> As the Father has loved me, so have I loved you. Now remain in my love. If you keep my commands, you will remain in my love, just as I have kept my Father's commands and remain in his love. I have told you this so that my joy may be in you and that your joy may be complete. My command is this: Love each other as I have loved you. Greater love has no one than this: to lay down one's life for one's friends.

In loving God above all else, and laying my life down for others, I live abundantly now while I'm storing up treasures that will last forever. Henry Drummond, author of *The Greatest Thing in the World*, said, "You will find as you look back upon your life that the moments when you have truly lived are the moments when you have done things in the spirit of love."[30]

Chapter 27

I Bow Down

I bow down to the One who bowed much further than me.
I bow down in the shadow of the darkened tree.
I can see much clearer from here.
Heaven is much nearer from here.

—JOHN WILLISON

When someone dear to us is suddenly gone from our life, it's easy to feel uncertain about the future and question God's goodness. This is a natural human reaction that can actually create an opportunity for God to reveal Himself to us like never before. He doesn't waste a moment of our sorrow; He uses it mercifully to draw us to Himself so we can truly see Him.

After Job lost his family and God met him in person, he realized that God was in control and had eternal purposes that he knew nothing about. He acknowledged, "I know that you can do all things; no purpose of yours can be thwarted. You asked, 'Who is this that obscures my plans without knowledge?' Surely I spoke of things I did not understand, things too wonderful for me to know" (Job 42:1–3).

He became aware of God's glorious, sovereign presence, which enabled him to see what he was made of: "My ears had heard of you but now my eyes have seen you. Therefore, I despise myself and repent in dust and ashes" (Job 42:5–6). Prior to Job's losses he knew about God, but now he *experienced* God. Before seeing God, Job questioned

Him. God gave Job more than answers; He gave Job Himself, the Answer to all we hope or dream about.

In another biblical story, we see Isaiah, who was a court prophet as well as King Uzziah's cousin. When the king died, Isaiah felt a huge loss. However, when he saw God on His throne, high and lifted up, he also saw what he was made of. "'Woe to me!' I cried. 'I am ruined! For I am a man of unclean lips, and I live among a people of unclean lips, and my eyes have seen the King, the Lord Almighty'" (Isaiah 6:5).

You'd think that when you *see* God, you'd immediately feel better. But that didn't happen with Job, Isaiah, or me. When we see God, we see our deficiencies. Like Isaiah and Job, I saw what I was made of—and my need to bow down. I saw how quickly I had been to doubt, enough to question God's goodness regardless of how much He had shown me in the past or present. I doubted God's goodness and justice, but He was never threatened by my questions. He remained sovereign, faithful, gracious, and compassionate because He does not change (Malachi 3:6).

Charles Spurgeon said, "God will never do anything with us … till he has first undone us."[31] My losses and struggles provided a gaping hole in my life, which made more space for God to fill me with His powerful presence and love. Becoming aware of God's presence is like being a diamond on a black cloth. When light (or God's presence) shines on us, every flaw is revealed. When our flaws are exposed, we have new awareness, and thus a new opportunity, for God to touch, reshape, and restore us. My story isn't exactly like Job's or Isaiah's, but my God is. The experience of seeing God, moved Job from despair to life. It moved Isaiah from sorrow to ministry. What He did for them, He will do for me—and for you—according to the unique story He's given each of us.

I have seen God high and lifted up, and I have also chosen to live and to love again.

One of the last movies Jessica and I watched together was *Finding Nemo*. While watching it again a few years ago, I saw a truth illustrated in the scene when Dory and Marlin are inside the whale.

In the beginning of the movie, Marlin's wife is killed by a barracuda after laying her eggs. Nemo, the only surviving egg, hatches and grows up. After experiencing over-protection because of his dad's fears, Nemo attempts to prove that he can swim on his own and be okay. However, he is captured in a fishing net and taken far away. His father Marlin then sets out across the ocean to find and rescue him, meeting Dory along the way. Marlin and Dory encounter struggle after struggle until they end up being swallowed by a whale.

When they are in the back of the whale's mouth, Dory exemplifies simple trust as she frolics on the waves in the whale's mouth and sings, "Just keep swimming! Just keep swimming!" Marlin, on the other hand, is beside himself with fear and falls to the floor of the whale's mouth, crying in despair.

The whale begins making sounds, and since Dory can speak "whale," she interprets what she thinks the whale is saying. "He either wants a rootbeer float, or he wants us to go to the back of his throat," she unassumingly tells Marlin. Of course Marlin concludes that the whale wants to digest them. As he holds tightly to the whale's tongue, Dory urges, "Marlin, the whale is telling you to 'Let go!'" Marlin fearfully calls back, "How do you know something bad isn't going to happen?" She answers, "I don't."[32] Dory lets go and Marlin hesitantly does too. To the back of the whale's throat they go, and they are conveniently sprayed into the ocean only to discover the whale has brought them exactly where they wanted to go.

The very thing Marlin thought would kill him, being swallowed by a whale, is what brought him to his desired destination. Lesson learned. Marlin let go and soon found Nemo. He learned to trust instead of speaking fear into every situation.

That's the point. Unfortunately, I found myself to be more like Marlin than Dory in my own circumstances. I had no control over my situation either—only mine was a true story. It was then I realized that just as Marlin's trouble (being inside the whale) brought him to shore where he found Nemo, my storm had also brought me to the shore I longed for: the shores of God's endless grace, strength, and love.

In the first couple years after the girls died, I had a series of dreams about tidal waves. The first dream had the most impact. I was riding a towering tsunami. Terrified, I thought for sure I would wipe out and be destroyed along with everything around me.

In my dream I realized that I was actually waterskiing a huge wave, behind a boat with a driver. Although still petrified I would wipe out, I realized that I only needed to hold on and trust the driver. As I approached land, I saw the driver was navigating with expert skill, and he brought me safely to shore.

When I landed, I observed devastation everywhere. Dead bodies and mourners were spread out with other debris along the shore. I felt helpless but began to comfort and pray for hurting individuals. I awoke from my dream sobbing, wondering what it all meant.

Subsequent dreams like it followed, but in those dreams I prayed with small groups of people. In time I came to see that it was my tsunami that actually brought me to shore. I had been pulled there, and the only effort required of me was to hold on to the rope and trust the driver of the boat.

Eventually, I understood the meaning of my recurring dream. As I have kept on in my journey of grief, drawing close to God in desperation, honesty, and responsiveness, God has produced the fruit of the Spirit in my life that comes as a result of knowing and experiencing Him in and through the storm. The people in my tsunami dream, others hurt by losses in life, are some of those who He's given me to nurture and care for. We all experience a crash of some sort, produced by the storms of life and are also given the opportunity to comfort others with the same comfort we've received from God.

Experiencing God's presence and light shining in and through the darkness of my storm has exposed my heart, requiring a deeper surrender to trust Him. As I've remembered the signs, I've become aware of God in many fresh, new ways. Because of His great love, I was not, and will not, be consumed. God is good; He is my portion, and I will seek Him and wait to receive His mercies, which are new every morn-ing (Lamentations 3:22–25).

As I bow down and worship in the presence of the One who bowed much further for me, I remain confident that I will see the goodness of the Lord in the land of the living. I will not cast away my confidence because I know my reward is God Himself. If I endure to the end, I will receive my lover's crown, which I will lay at His feet when I bow down in His eternal love and presence.

~ Chapter 28 ~

My House Still Stands

Of one thing I am perfectly sure:
God's story never ends with ashes.
—*These Strange Ashes* by Elisabeth Elliot

God is sovereign. He is in control, but that does not mean He controls everything. Part of the sovereignty of God means that nothing is outside His providence or catches Him off guard. God is always reaching out with His plan of redemption to redeem our pain and loss, whether from poor choices of ours, or of others, or from circumstances beyond anyone's control.

The very things with potential to destroy us can actually be what strengthen us. In the story of Joseph, his words to his brothers illustrate this truth: "You meant this thing for evil, but the Lord intended it for good" (Genesis 50:20). No matter what our circumstances and trials may be, God is still good and always will be. We may not end up on a throne like Joseph, but our house will still stand if our foundation is built on the Rock Jesus Christ and we look to God.

As a child of God, I know that any evil that befalls me has been allowed by Him. I am not a victim of some random act of misfortune. But neither has God overlooked me. He has eternal purposes in all that He allows, working everything together for good for those who love Him.

Throughout Scripture, God has promised to vindicate His people,

216

and while reading Isaiah 54:17, I sensed God's personal promise to me: "'No weapon forged against you will prevail, and you will refute every tongue that accuses you. This is the heritage of the servants of the LORD, and this is their vindication from me,' declares the LORD."

Once at a prayer meeting early in my grief journey, I received prayer from a man who knew nothing about me, my loss, or my struggle. As he prayed, he said that God would vindicate me to my accusers. I didn't understand what that meant, but I knew who my accusers were. My own wrong thinking patterns and the devil's lies— what the enemy said about me and about God: *You are a loser. You did something wrong. God can't really love you. He's really not good or just.* But just as Job was vindicated to his accusers (his three wrongly opinionated friends), the Lord has also vindicated me. He's done this by revealing Himself through His constant presence, affirming me in His love, and speaking truth in the midst of my unbelief.

A major vindication came from the Lord as I read a sermon by Charles Spurgeon that deeply touched me. His uplifting words became God's words to my heart and healed me, addressing remnants of the ugly lie that I was a loser. But God cut that lie off at its root. His work is perfect, and when He declares a thing to be done, it's done. Spurgeon wrote:

> Believers shall never be losers by God. ... Shall you lose anything by what you give to God? Never! Depend on it; He will be no man's debtor. There dwells not on earth or heaven any man who shall be a creditor to the Most High. The best investment a man makes is that which he gives to the Lord from a right motive. Nothing is lost which is offered to the cause of God.[33]

God then reminded me of an experience I had with Him while camping with a close friend in the mountains years ago. One morning we went off individually to each pray for our children. I set out for the summit, making it a literal mountaintop experience, and began my time with God by singing "I Surrender All."

Joey was at a pivotal crossroads in his teens at the time, and I was seeking God on his behalf. God emphasized the Scripture I read during that time by directing me to give not just Joey, but all my children, back to Him. "Anyone who loves their son or daughter more than me is not worthy of me" (Matthew 10:37).

The words went deep, and I wept as I gave my kids to the Lord that day on the mountain. I can only imagine what it may have been like for Abraham to offer up Isaac on a real stone altar. Since then, I've heard someone say that God never wanted Isaac's life. He wanted Abraham's heart, just as He wanted mine. When I returned to our camper that day, God had given my friend the same Scripture to pray for me.

That morning on the mountain, I gave my children back to the Lord, realizing they were not mine to begin with, committing them to Him and the work of His kingdom.

I am not a loser! I gave my kids back to the Lord. They are His. I did not lose them. I know just where they are. A quote by Jim Elliot, a renowned missionary who was martyred for his faith, captures this very truth: "He is no fool who gives what he cannot keep, to gain that which he cannot lose."[34]

About a year before the accident, I went to a baby shower with Jessica. Shortly after the accident, the friend hosting the shower sent me a picture that she had found of Jess and me. There on the bookshelf directly behind us sat a book titled *Losing to Gain*. God vindicated me from my accusers with this revelation.

I believe my act of surrender on that Colorado mountaintop was also an act of storing up treasures in heaven that I will have for eternity.

"Gazing at Jesus and glancing at my problems" is what a friend of mine recently said she was doing while facing a serious problem. My heart resonated with her statement. I recalled the image God had showed me, at Joey's and Bree's wedding, about fixing my eyes on Jesus (Hebrews 12:2). When Bree walked down the aisle, her face matched Joey's with anticipation. Love and excitement emanated from her eyes as she saw only him. She was a beautiful, radiant bride.

Nothing could distract her from her bridegroom. What a beautiful image of "gazing at Jesus." No distractions.

To gaze or fix my eyes on one thing means I must turn away from something else.

As I gaze into God's Word, my losses and struggles fade into the light of His truth. When I meditate on His truths, I store up treasures in my heart, and as I spend time in His presence, I can go forward with confidence and hope, assured of His goodness and love.

That does not mean ignoring the problems, losses, struggles, and disappointments of life. Rather, it means allowing them to become stepping stones in my journey to the high places of His eternal love—instead of allowing them to become stumbling blocks that destroy my relationship with Him and others.

I once heard it said that the only way to avoid grief is never to love. By lingering in the negative emotions of grief, we numb the positive emotions as well and close our hearts to love. This unhealthy response creates a stumbling block where one falls into a life of isolation and loneliness. Although my heart still aches for my girls, my love for them compels me to long for heaven. This longing has actually become a stepping stone for me to press on and travel my journey here until I am home with them in heaven.

Until then, I rejoice that my house still stands because of the foundation I have in Christ, the Rock of my salvation. "Though the mountains be shaken and the hills [which are temporary] be removed, my Maker and Husband has promised that His unfailing love for me [which is eternal] will not be shaken or His covenant of peace be removed" (Isaiah 54:10). My Shepherd who knows me intimately has caused me to rejoice in knowing that goodness and mercy will follow me all the days of my life and I will dwell in the house of the Lord forever! (Psalm 23:6). That ... is life eternal.

Nikki's art teacher gave me a painting Nikki made. Her assignment was to replicate a painting of their choice, and Nikki chose to paint a house. When I saw it, I immediately went back to the Scripture God gave me for our family when the kids were young: "By wisdom a house is built; and through understanding it is established; through knowledge its rooms are filled with rare and beautiful treasures" (Proverbs 24:3–4).

Although no two families will look alike, this Scripture promises that the results will be a family that offers "rare and beautiful treasures" to the world. Since true beauty reflects the character of God and not our own goodness, there is no way to fake this. It must be the result of building on the Rock—life's surest foundation. My house still stands.

Nikki's replica painting of House
Paysage, Mont-roig by Joan Miro

Chapter 29

The Bride of Christ

For your Maker is your husband—
the Lord Almighty is his name—
the Holy One of Israel is your Redeemer.
—Isaiah 54:5

There is still so much about God I will never understand until I
have been with Him ten thousand years, as the hymn says—and
then I'll continue to discover more after that. I can honestly say that
the older I get, the less I understand why He allows certain things
to happen. I think that's because He has become bigger to me, and I
have become smaller. That's a good thing. I *know* that His ways are
past finding out (Romans 11:33). But to the degree I don't understand the whys, I have come to trust and experience His boundless
love for me as His beloved, His bride.

Because God personally gave me the eternal bridal theme early
in my Christian walk and then confirmed it again with the picture of
the bride and groom from Bree the very day my girls became brides
in heaven, and again through the picture of my girls as brides, I read
up on the ancient Jewish wedding practices. Understanding these
just a little bit has given me a clearer picture of the covenant Jesus
has made not only with me but also with the church as His bride.

Picture Joey gave Debbie on the day the girls became brides in heaven

The Bridegroom Returns, copyright Jennifer Oakley-Delaplante
www.jenniferoakley-delaplante.com

First, the father chose a bride for his son. We are told in Ephesians 1:4 that God the Father chose us, before the creation of the world, to be holy and blameless in His sight. John 15:16 says that we did not choose Him, but He chose us. Since the beginning, God has always initiated a relationship with mankind, but it is our choice to respond by loving Him above all else.

222

Next, the father of the groom paid a price for the bride-to-be. This was something of great worth that reflected how much she was valued. We are told that the heavenly Father valued us so much that He gave His only Son for us. I know that I have not been redeemed with perishable things, but with the precious blood of Christ, as told in 1 Peter 1:18–19. Because I am greatly valued, Jesus poured out His lifeblood in payment for me—and for you. We are told in Hebrews 12:2 that it was for the joy set before Him that He endured the cross. Besides His obedience to the Father, each one of us was part of that joy set before Him.

Another step in this betrothal was the bridal pledge-gift from the groom. He would pledge to fulfill His promise of marriage. Second Corinthians 5 talks about our eternal dwelling, and in verse 5 says, "Now the one who has fashioned us for this very purpose [dwelling eternally] is God, who has given us the Spirit as a deposit, guaranteeing what is to come." As the bride of Christ, we receive the Holy Spirit as our engagement ring, as the groom's pledge, to guarantee what is to come. As His bride, I gladly show off my engagement ring by listening to and obeying the Holy Spirit and loving others.

The next step in this ancient espousal was a bridal contract, a written agreement the bride received that stated all the groom's promises to her, and what her part in the agreement was to be. She had to read it and sign it. Although she was chosen, she still had a choice to agree or not. We, as the bride of Christ, have also been given great and precious promises so that through them we may participate in the divine nature (2 Peter 1:4). I daily read this love letter from God (His Word) and meditate on it to know what is included in His covenant of love to me, and how I can fulfill my part and appropriate it to my life.

When I received love letters from Joe while we were engaged, I read and re-read them to remember his words. How much more with our heavenly Bridegroom?

Finally, the groom goes away to prepare their future home, including the wedding chamber. The bride, not knowing when he will return, prepares herself and waits for him with expectancy. In John

14:3, Jesus explained He was going away to prepare a place for us and that He will come again to receive us to Himself. I imagine what my home in heaven will be like and anticipate spending eternity there. Luke 12:40 tells us that we must be ready because He will come at an hour when we don't expect Him.

Just as the bride and groom were separated during their betrothal period until the wedding, so are we, the bride of Christ. We are betrothed and waiting with great anticipation for the day we will be united with Jesus, our Bridegroom. The full intimacy we so greatly long for will not happen until He returns, but during this waiting time, we can actively prepare ourselves.

One of the ways I prepare myself for His return is by not allowing my feelings or circumstances to dictate how I relate to Him or others. I wear the pledge of the Holy Spirit, and walk in God's light, step by step, keeping His covenant of love alive in my heart. Corrie ten Boom said, "If you look at the world you'll be distressed. If you look within you'll be depressed. If you look at God, you'll be at rest." She confidently declared: "There is no panic in Heaven. God has no problems, only plans."[35]

When I fix my eyes on Jesus, my Bridegroom, I rise above my circumstances and sit with Him in heavenly places, knowing that nothing can separate me from His love. I will also be ready when Jesus comes, because I've turned from lesser loves, whether they be losses or gains, disallowing anything to come before my relationship with Him. Intimacy with Him is my greatest desire.

God invites us to partner with Him in loving others. But He often allows unwanted circumstances to linger in our lives to reveal our need for dependence on Him. The lingering darkness in my life stirred up a fight in my spirit that declared, *Enough! I will contend for life and truth, for that which is eternal.*

God wants our hearts. He delights in partnering with us because that's what we we're made for, and that's what brings us true joy as His betrothed bride! Whether it is to stand with the helpless, to comfort the hurting, to seek and find the lost, to nurture babes to maturity, or to simply to care for people we know, we are called to live a life of love.

I have had different seasons of what that expression of love looks like. Presently, I am making eternal investments in the lives of little ones. I have been teaching a two-year-old Sunday school class for several years, knowing that I am laying a foundation in children's lives that will impact their future relationships with God.

I also am investing in my granddaughter, Vivien, who I watch one day a week. For nearly five years I've had precious, quality one-on-one time with her at least once a week. I'm not only enjoying and building a relationship with her, but I'm also planting seeds of truth in her young, fertile heart that will affect her relationship with Jesus, her heavenly Bridegroom. Besides her, I love to spend time with my grand-niece Aubree and nephew Ryder and consider these two children to be precious and eternal investments as well.

I love singing and playing guitar at a senior memory care home where I minister to the spirit and enter the fragile world of the elderly, inviting them to encounter the comfort and joy of God's presence in a way that only music can. My prayer is to help them to both discover and remember the life God has placed inside of them, so they can experience His peace and presence until they are called to heaven.

Joe and I have been leading a grief group at our church for the past three years. I look at these people as the ones in my tsunami dream. I've ministered to them in a group setting as well as one-on-one, comforting them with the same compassion I've received. I have also been able to minister to others who have experienced grief, and the many dimensions of it, because of what I've walked through.

During grief, many secondary issues arise that may have been buried until the rawness of bereavement exposes them, as I have experienced. These issues aren't grief itself, and yet are an opportunity for people to apply the truths and principles of God's Word, for revelation, healing, and freedom as they navigate through their painful journey.

Joey and Bree are doing well as they also press on and trust in God's faithfulness. They love the relationships they have at a church they helped start, where Joey is a staff pastor and Bree is the worship director. They enjoy life with their daughter, Vivien. They've had their ups and downs, struggles and victories, but—just like Joe and I—they've learned to contend for, expect, and believe in the goodness of God.

I've come to see that the areas of our greatest wounds and struggles are the places of greatest ministry. Jesus' message was the loudest where He hurt the most—the cross—and so is ours.

The enemy may try to stifle, distort, and defeat the purposes of God in our lives, but God makes good come from it every time if we embrace it. He's the Redeemer. He takes the very things the enemy intended for our destruction and uses them to bring life to us and to others.

I have learned that the moments that have truly defined me have been those moments alone with God. It has been in these moments of desperation and struggle that God has gently whispered secrets to my heart. The occasions may have been messy and even repelling to my flesh—moments that have required surrender of my inner self, calling me back into my story, inviting me back into life. I have not gained anything by avoiding my pain; I've gained much by embracing it.

God speaks truth, and His truth sets us free. We often have immediate peace, but that does not mean that we see immediate results. We are on a journey full of twists and turns and ups and downs—a journey that is only progressive as we follow truth and allow patience to have its perfect way in us.

We must remember we are eternal beings headed for an eternal home, and we must not become too attached to our temporary dwelling. We are told that at just the right time, God will make everything beautiful (Ecclesiastes 3:11).

Pierre Teilhard de Chardin said, "We are not human beings having a spiritual experience, but we are spiritual beings having a human experience."[36] Vance Havner said it like this: "If you are a Christian, you are not a citizen of this world trying to get to Heaven; you are a citizen of Heaven making your way through this world."[37]

As the bride of Christ, I look forward my final destination, where my real home is, and how the real story ends. "But our citizenship is in heaven. And we eagerly await a Savior from there, the Lord Jesus Christ, who, by the power that enables him to bring everything under his control, will transform our lowly bodies so that they will be like his glorious body" (Philippians 3:20–22).

Years ago, my cousin and her husband moved to receive their US Army training. I asked her if she was settled in, and she replied, "No, this is only temporary. It's not my real home."

Her statement quickened truth in me. That is precisely how I should think about life here. My real citizenship is in heaven: "For he was looking forward to the city with foundations, whose architect and builder is God" (Hebrews 11:10). I need to look beyond this life to receive the motivation needed to continue moving forward in my healing. As Abraham looked to a better country, so can I.

I believe my daughters and the rest of the church in heaven are calling out, "The Spirit and the bride say, 'Come!'" (Revelation 22:17). And when the Bridegroom returns, we will rejoice with the church triumphant and sing, "Let us rejoice and be glad and give him glory! For the wedding of the Lamb has come, and his bride has made herself ready" (Revelation 19:7)

Three brides in heaven

Chapter 30

Still Being Written

It's not about now, it's not about here
It's all about then when there's nothing to fear
It's all about then, there—the mystery's clear
When then will be now, and there will be here.

—Gloria Gaither

The purpose of this book was not to encounter Debbie Mayer. My desire was to share God's heart, power, and love in the midst of great loss and struggle. Wherever you are in life and whatever your circumstances, God is in the here and now while eternity awaits you.

Everyone ever born has a story to live. In each story, God reaches out, offering life and love in ways we can grasp. God encounters, lessons, and healing of grief will not be exactly the same for everyone. However, the outcome will be—hope, healing, and a good future. I trust my story has encouraged others to not give up, but to look to God. When we are hurting, God hurts with us—waiting for us to turn to Him and His Word.

God wants to provide an eternity of love and freedom to everyone and is especially sensitive to those who are broken. We are the ones He searches for, longing to give Himself. He is the Good Shepherd in pursuit of the hurting; He'll find them, carry them, and hold them close to His heart. But it is only in relationship with Jesus Christ that we can know how much God is for us and not against us.

The night my girls died, I realized how important it is not to think of eternal life as something that happens when we die, but to think about it right now. Jesus described eternal life as knowing Him—now. He said, "Now this is eternal life: that they know you, the only true God, and Jesus Christ, whom you have sent" (John 17:3).

Our eternal life begins the moment we put our faith in Jesus Christ, and it cannot be interrupted by physical death: "Very truly I tell you, whoever hears my word and believes him who sent me has eternal life and will not be judged but has crossed over from death to life" (John 5:24). Life apart from Jesus is spiritual death: "For the wages of sin is death, but the gift of God is eternal life in Christ Jesus our Lord" (Romans 6:23). Physical death is not our biggest problem; it's our sin and its consequences of separation from God. But for a believer, Jesus is as close as our own breath.

My girls are not in heaven because they were good enough. Our hope for heaven has nothing to do with deserving to go there, nor is salvation based on our good works. Quite the opposite. Christ died for broken sinners, paying the penalty for sin through His shed blood. Jesus suffered, died, was buried, and arose from the grave. The very moment we put our trust in Jesus is our first moment in eternity.

Shortly after the girls died, a friend of ours wrote this poem for us, describing this journey our girls experienced. It is titled "Author! Author!" by Craig Affeldt.

They've laid down their pens now, these three wonderful daughters
Writing the stories of their storybook lives.
No more time for helpful suggestions from family and friends.
No more time to correct the grammar, and fix the punctuation.
Their assignments are finished.

And, Oh! What books they were!
The first, nineteen chapters long,
Of a young woman, loving and caring, blossoming into adulthood.
The second, seventeen chapters, about a girl,
Navigating her way through the years of discovery;

And the third, only twelve chapters long,
Full of fun and excitement, just getting to the good parts.
And now, coming together, with featured roles in yet another chapter.
The way it is meant to be in storybook lives, in storybook families.

Then, we turn the page. The chapters end.
What sadness! What disappointment!
How we loved reading these books!
How we devoured each page, each sentence.
How we miss reading these chapters.
These wonderful books. These storybook lives.

Yet, we remember. We know. These books are still being written.
The Great Author has picked up their pens.
They are writing with His help now.
No need for helpful suggestions from family and friends.
No need to correct the grammar or fix the punctuation.
New, perfect chapters being written each day, for all eternity.
Full of fun and excitement.
Far more wonderful than we could ever imagine.
Full of discoveries far beyond our understanding.
Loving and caring beyond our human powers.
Each day and for eternity,
new chapters written in these storybook lives.

How we wish we could read these new stories!
Yet we remember. We know.
We will read these books one day.
Before you know it, we will be together again.
Reading these chapters. Together. For all eternity.
But not until we have finished our own assignments,
Writing the chapters of our own stories. Our own lives.
Until then, we remember,
"Let us fix our eyes on Jesus,
the author and perfecter of our faith."

God knows our life story from beginning to end. He's the author, but, as Craig's poem states, we are co-authors. We can finish our assignments and co-write the chapters of our own stories, inspired by the great Author of Life as we fix our eyes on Jesus, the perfecter of our faith.

It's important not to despise our story, but rather to read it. I have found it encouraging to trace what God has spoken throughout my life narrative and find a key theme in my story. In doing that, I've come to understand who I am and my life message better.

God wants us to hear His voice. He has fashioned each of our souls uniquely in how we experience and relate to Him. The way we connect with God is individual. We may be drawn close to Him through nature, music, journaling, listening to sermons or Bible studies, memorizing Scripture, or other ways. As a result, joy and thanksgiving will come to us as naturally as breathing.

As we remember our past, we can see how God has invited us to a compelling future. He likes to give us fresh insights. God is generous and loves to speak our language. He wants us to know His heart, and He's an expert at revealing His particular love to each of us.

Knowing God is not meant to be a mystery. Anyone can start by establishing a foundation built on the solid Rock of Jesus Christ. By believing in Him and looking to Him for salvation and guidance in life, we begin to know Him and, and with the Holy Spirit, we gain spiritual understanding. When we know God and His personal love, we then begin to discover who we really are. His beloved. God has so much for us: peace, rest, hope, healing, and most of all, love.

God meets us in our pain, exposing our wrong perceptions we may have of Him and ourselves. All we need to do is fix our gaze on Jesus and look at the unseen realities of heaven. He shows us even deeper aspects of His love, as we journey with Him in life, bringing us closer to Him and to others. The more we know God in relationship, the more we will reflect His image and character. This process will continue until we are with Him in heaven.

⤳

Recently Joe and I took a walk to enjoy the fall leaves. As I lamented the warm summer coming to an end, I couldn't help but embrace the kaleidoscope of autumn colors around me. It occurred to me that the changes in the leaves preserve the tree so that in the spring it can produce new life. Each season has its unique purpose and beauty. Similarly, seasons and changes in our own lives preserve and produce new life for us, with new meaning and beauty. Once we embrace God's eternal purpose, we can then embrace the beauty as well—and truly live.

A big part of this continuing process of life and healing is to move from receiving comfort to giving it. That is how we were designed to function, and yet apart from God's love, it's hard to climb out of ourselves. It is in giving that we receive, which is a continuing cycle of receiving God's love and then giving it out.

God rescued me from being ruled by feelings, where I lived for so long in the past. He has brought me to a place where I can hold my grief and pain in one hand, and my victory and healing in the other, where they are indelibly linked to His signature of love on my soul.

God continues to expand my eternal perspective into deeper dimensions of His love, establishing new ways for me to relate to Him and others. This is, after all, a journey of love and intimacy with God.

When my kids were quite young, I sensed God telling me that He would use our family to share His message of love. When the girls died, that dream died. But He has now shown me that we are doing that very thing. Through this book and through our story, our family continues to speak of God's great love, redemption, and faithfulness.

My story on earth is not over yet, nor is anyone's story here finished until God calls them home. Job suffered much and lost dear ones, but his last days were more blessed than his first. Proverbs 4:18 promises, "The path of the righteous is like the morning sun, shining ever brighter till the full light of day." When we are made righteous by God, we will shine brighter and brighter until that which is perfect comes.

I know who my God is, who I am, and where I'm going, where my eternal story will continue to shine. I will keep believing and proclaiming His goodness until the day I meet Jesus, my Bridegroom, face-to-face. Until then, "For me to live is Christ, and to die is gain" (Philippians 1:21).

Lord Jesus, I am Yours, Your beloved, Your bride.
I long to look into Your eyes on that final day.
Until then, I now declare,
"I am Yours, eternally Yours!"

Nikki, Krista, Bree, and Jess trying
on dresses for wedding – 2003

Bree, Joey, Nikki, and Krista – 2002

Joey and Jess – 2003

Bree and Jess – 2003

Krista, Nikki, Jess, and Debbie imitating Buddy's crooked smile

Jess, Krista, Nikki, and Joe after water ride on last vacation

Jess, Krista, Nikki, and Debbie on last vacation

Nikki, Joe, Debbie, Krista, and Jess in Florida on last vacation

Family photo – 2003

Krista – 2003

Nikki – 2003

Jessica and Buddy – 2003

Krista, Nikki, and Jessica – 2003

Our Sorrow, Our Love, Our Hope

Picture designed and given by Steve Darula

Notes

1   John Piper, "Dying for the Glory of Christ," *Desiring God*, November 3, 2004, accessed August 28, 2017, http://www.desiringgod.org/articles/dying-for-the-glory-of-christ.

2   C. S. Lewis, *The Complete C. S. Lewis Signature Classics* (San Francisco: HarperCollins, 2002), 448.

3   Ibid., 642.

4   Debbie McDaniel, "40 Inspiring Quotes from Elisabeth Elliot," *Crosswalk*, June 17, 2015, accessed August 29, 2017, http://www.crosswalk.com/faith/spiritual-life/inspiring-quotes/40-inspiring-quotes-from-elisabeth-elliot.html.

5   George McDonald, *Sir Gibbie* (London: J. M. Dent and Sons, 1911), 152.

6   Bill and Gloria Gaither, *Heaven* (Nashville: Thomas Nelson, 2003), 16.

7   Corrie ten Boom, *The Hiding Place* (Grand Rapids: Baker Publishing Group), 17.

8   Hannah Hurnard, *Hinds' Feet on High Places* (Carol Stream, IL: Tyndale House, 1979), 65.

9   Chambers, "The Discipline Of Difficulty," *My Utmost for His Highest*, August 2 reading, accessed August 29, 2017, https://utmost.org/classic/the-discipline-of-difficulty-classic/.

10 *Oxford Living Dictionary*, s.v. "courage," accessed August 29, 2017, https://en.oxforddictionaries.com/definition/courage.

11 Gaither, *Heaven*, 54.

12 "Vance Havner > Quotes > Quotable Quotes," *Goodreads*, accessed September 2, 2017, https://www.goodreads.com/quotes/234479-if-you-are-a-christian-you-are-not-a-citizen.

13 L. B. Cowman, *Streams in the Desert* (Grand Rapids: Zondervan, 2010), 317.

14 A. W. Tozer, *The Pursuit of God* (New York: Start Publishing, 2013), 52.

15 Lewis, *A Grief Observed* (New York: HarperOne, 1994), 3.

16 Lewis, *The Silver Chair* (New York: HarperCollins, 2005), 27.

17 Strong's Concordance, s.v. "#3341, *metanoia*," BibleHub, accessed September 2, 2017, http://biblehub.com/greek/3341.htm.

18 Rick Warren, "Eliminate Negative Self-Talk," Pastor Rick's Daily Hope, May 21, 2014, accessed August 29, 2017, http://pastorrick.com/devotional/english/eliminate-negative-self-talk_255.

19 The Treasury of David Commentary, Bible Study Tools, Psalm 42:5 exposition, accessed August 29, 2017, http://www.biblestudytools.com/commentaries/treasury-of-david/psalms-42-5.html.

20 Chambers, "The Discipline Of Difficulty," My Utmost for His Highest, August 2 reading, accessed August 29, 2017, https://utmost.org/classic/the-discipline-of-difficulty-classic/.

21 Oxford Living Dictionary, s.v. "courage," accessed August 29, 2017, https://en.oxford dictionaries.com/definition/courage.

22 Jerry Sittser, *A Grace Disguised: How the Soul Grows through Loss* (Grand Rapids: Zondervan, 2009), 85.

23 Henri Nouwen, *Spiritual Direction: Wisdom for the Long Walk of Faith* (New York: Harper One, 2006), 32–34.

24 Mary Rourke, "Spiritual Strategy: Rebuilding: Father Henri Nouwen specializes in giving direction to troubled flocks. Recently, he outlined how L.A. could get past the riots," *Los Angeles Times*, October 8, 1992, accessed September 2, 2017, http://articles.latimes.com /1992-10-08/news/vw-741_1_henri-nouwen.

25 "Norman Cousins Quotes," *BrainyQuote*, accessed August 30, 2017, https://www.brainy quote.com/quotes/quotes/n/normancous121747.html.

26 Tim Jackson, "How Can I Live With My Loss?" RBC.org, accessed September 2, 2017, http://web001.rbc.org/pdf/discovery-series/how-can-i-live-with-my-loss.pdf.

27 A. W. Tozer, "Why Be a Mediocre Christian?" sermon, Avenue Road Alliance Church, Toronto.

28 C. S. Lewis, *Made for Heaven: And Why on Earth It Matters* (New York: HarperCollins, 2009), 57–58.

29 Kurt Bruner and Jim Ware, *Finding God in The Lord of the Rings* (Carol Stream, IL: Tyndale House, 2001), 44.

30 "Henry Drummond > Quotes," *Goodreads*, accessed August 30, 2017, https://www. goodreads.com/author/quotes/59853.Henry_Drummond.

31 Charles Spurgeon, "The Divine Call for Missionaries," Christian Classics Ethereal Library, accessed August 30, 2017, http://www.ccel.org/ccel/spurgeon/sermons23.xxi.html.

32 "Finding Dory (2016)," *IMDb*, accessed August 30, 2017, http://www.imdb.com/title /tt2277860/.

33 Spurgeon, "The Turning of Job's Captivity," Christian Classics Ethereal Library, accessed August 30, 2017, http://www.ccel.org/ccel/spurgeon/sermons21.liii.html.

34 Elisabeth Elliot, *Shadow of the Almighty: The Life and Testament of Jim Elliot* (Peabody, MA: Hendrickson Publishers, 1958), 11.

35 "Corrie ten Boom > Quotes," *Goodreads*, accessed August 30, 2017, https://www. goodreads.com/author/quotes/102203.Corrie_ten_Boom.

36 Gaither, Heaven, 54.

37 "Vance Havner > Quotes > Quotable Quotes," *Goodreads*, accessed September 2, 2017, https://www.goodreads.com/quotes/234479-if-you-are-a-christian-you-are-not-a-citizen.